Bookkeeping Goldmine

Unlocking **six-Figure** success from home

By

William M. Upshaw

Copyright © 2024 William M. Upshaw

All rights reserved. No part of this book may be reproduced transmitted in any form or by any means, electronic, or mechanical, including photocopying, recording, or by any information storage and retrieval system, without written permission from the author, accept by a reviewer who may summarize brief passages in a review.

Disclaimer

This book intended to provide our readers with information and motivation. It is a sold with the knowledge that the publisher is not engaged to provide any form of psychological, legal, or other professional advice. Each page's content is the sold expression and opinion of the author. Neither the publisher not the individual author (s) shall be responsible for any physical, psychological, emotional, financial, or commercial damages, including but not limited to special, incidental, consequential, or other damages. Our point of view and rights are the same: you are solely accountable for your decisions, actions, and outcomes.

Table of contents

Disclaimer...3

Introduction:..7
   Uncovering the Accounting Treasure 7

Chapter 1:..13
   Bookkeeping Fundamentals...................................13
   1.1 Clarifying Bookkeeping:......................................17
   Its Nature and Importance......................................17
   1.2 Crucial Knowledge and Requirements for Future Bookkeepers...23
   1.3 Managing Law and Regulation Needs...............28

Chapter 2:..34
   Setting Up Your Home Office 34
   2.1 Creating an Ergonomic and Productive Workspace.........38
   2.2 Choosing the Appropriate Hardware and Software.........42
   2.3 Setting Up Effective Processes and Mechanisms 47

Chapter 3:..51
   Establishing Your Brand...51
   3.1 Developing Your Unique Selling Proposition....57
   3.2 Creating an Engaging Brand Identity.................64
   3.3 Marketing Strategies to Attract Clients 69

Chapter 4:..74
   Becoming Proficient in Bookkeeping Fundamentals......74
   4.1 Understanding Financial Statements: Balance Sheets, Income Statements, and Cash Flow Statements.....................79

Chapter 4.2: Recording Transactions and Maintaining Accurate Records 89

4.3 Introduction to Accounting Software: Enhancing Efficiency with Useful Tips and Tricks...98

Chapter 5:...107

Managing Clients...107

5.1 Onboarding Clients: Establishing Expectations and Agreements...114

5.2 Communication Strategies for Developing Solid Client Relationships..121

5.3 Dealing with Challenging Clients and Resolving Conflicts in a Professional Manner 129

Chapter 6:...138

Growing Your Business...138

6.1 Enhancing Operational Efficiency for Business Expansion 147

6.2 Hiring Assistance: Virtual Assistants, Contractors, and Employees...154

6.3 Expanding Your Service Offerings and Reaching New Customers..160

Chapter 7:...168

Maximizing Profitability 168

7.1 Strategically Pricing Your Services...................175

7.2 Implementing Efficient Time Management Techniques 183

7.3 Maximizing Efficiency and Boosting Profit Margins through Technology...191

Chapter 8:...199

Conquering Obstacles and Avoiding Traps...........199

8.1 Common Mistakes to Avoid in a Bookkeeping Business 207

8.2 Managing Burnout and Maintaining Work-Life Balance 214

8.3 Adapting to Industry Changes and Economic Shifts 222

Chapter 9: 230

Future Trends in Bookkeeping Like 230

9.1 Embracing Automation and Artificial Intelligence 237

9.2 The Emergence of Remote Work and Virtual Bookkeeping Services 245

9.3 Opportunities for Innovation and Growth in the Industry 256

Appendix: More Tools and Resources for Bookkeepers 293

4. In conclusion 322

Introduction:

Uncovering the Accounting Treasure

Amelia lived in the quiet town of Willow Brook, surrounded by rolling hills and streams. Though she possessed many talents, none were as impressive as her natural aptitude for mathematics. Amelia was enthralled with the grace and accuracy of mathematical equations from an early age when other kids could barely do simple arithmetic. It seemed as though the language of numbers incomprehensibly communicated with her.

Amelia's love of numbers developed into a zealous quest for knowledge as she grew older. She devoured accounting and finance books, eager to absorb the knowledge they held. She was confident that she would devote herself to the honorable bookkeeping profession when it came time to make her plans.

Amelia's journey started when she joined a prominent university, where she studied under renowned academics to perfect her skills. She enthusiastically soaked in every bit of information that came her way as she submerged herself in the world of ledgers and balance sheets. And she believed she was prepared to take on the world as she emerged with her diploma.

Amelia worked hard and persevered for years in the prestigious world of corporate finance, moving up the success ladder. She was successful and received recognition, yet she still felt something needed to be added. She seemed to lack something as if she were searching for something more purposeful and satisfying.

Then, inspiration came like a lightning bolt on that fateful day as she sat looking out of her office window at the bustling metropolis below. What if she wondered to herself if she could use her knowledge of accountancy to make something unique?

What if she could create her route to success and escape the bonds of corporate servitude?

Amelia set out on a mission to discover the undiscovered benefits of entrepreneurship and carve out a niche for herself in remote bookkeeping, driven by a renewed sense of purpose. This led to the creation of the Bookkeeping Goldmine, a ray of hope and opportunity for budding business owners looking to forge their path in the enormous world of commerce.

You might wonder, though, what the Bookkeeping Goldmine is. It is more than just a company; it represents liberty, an example of the strength of tenacity, and a doorway to immense wealth. The journey we will take together in the following pages will reveal the keys to creating a profitable home-based bookkeeping business hidden within its ancient corridors.

We'll unearth a plethora of information and understanding from our investigation of the

Bookkeeping Goldmine that can help you on your journey to success. We will only stop once we have mastered bookkeeping fundamentals and laid the foundation for your business. We are committed to achieving entrepreneurial greatness.

But let's pause to consider the endless possibilities of a home-based bookkeeping firm before we continue with our quest. If you would, picture yourself living a life in which you are in control of your fate, free from the restrictions of regular nine-to-five work and able to pursue your own business from the comforts of home.

There are countless prospects for prospective entrepreneurs in today's fast-paced, constantly evolving world. There's never been a better moment to take control of your destiny and set off on an incredible trip than now, with the rise of remote employment and the rising demand for financial services.

But make no mistake: starting an accounting business from home is complex. It calls for bravery, tenacity, and an openness to the unknown. However, the benefits can be remarkable for those with the guts to follow their entrepreneurial calling.

Are you prepared to go on this exciting journey with us, dear reader? Are you ready to follow Amelia on her journey to find the Bookkeeping Goldmine's hidden secrets and pave your route to success? If this is the case, you should answer the call of adventure since what lies ahead seems impressive.

We will explore the nuances of starting and expanding a home-based bookkeeping firm in the upcoming chapters, covering everything from establishing a home office to becoming proficient in client administration. We will give lessons learned from Amelia's Personal experiences navigating the highs and lows of entrepreneurship as we travel through her tales of triumph and adversity.

However, let's consider the limitless possibilities within the Bookkeeping Goldmine before we set out on our quest because the opportunities in the field of remote bookkeeping are virtually boundless, as are the rewards. So, reader, muster your bravery and get ready to reveal the hidden gems waiting for you. This is where the adventure starts.

Chapter 1:

Bookkeeping Fundamentals

A young woman named Sarah lived in the vibrant metropolis of Motorville, where the skyline kissed the heavens and the streets hummed with energy. Sarah had just received her degree in accounting from the esteemed Motorville University and was driven by ambition. She had always been drawn to the realm of numbers because, during the chaos around her, she found comfort in their accuracy and rationality.

Sarah was at a loss about what to do after graduating from college. After years of refining her techniques and immersing herself in the complexities of financial theory, she was now confronted with the enormous challenge of putting her knowledge to use in the real world. She eagerly accepted the challenge, wanting to establish herself in the cutthroat world of corporate finance.

Sarah soon understood the value of having a solid foundation in bookkeeping as she dug deeper into the accounting field.

The careful record-keeping process was the cornerstone of any successful business, upon which all financial transactions hinged. She realized that without a firm grasp of bookkeeping fundamentals, she would be lost in a sea of numbers and unable to handle the intricacies of the financial industry.

Thus, Sarah embarked on a mission to learn the bookkeeping trade secrets, a voyage that would lead her to the core of financial management and establish the foundation for her future achievements. She read books about it nonstop, eagerly taking in all the pearls of knowledge they offered. She was eager to learn from those who had gone before her and sought out mentors and subject matter experts. Most crucial, though, was that she rolled up her sleeves, went to work, and learned from her mistakes by using her newly acquired knowledge in practical situations.

Sarah learned from her experience that the fundamentals of bookkeeping rested on a few fundamental ideas, all of which are critical to the success of any aspirant business owner or accountant.

The first of these guidelines was correctness, the foundation for all financial records. Sarah realized that any analysis or decision-making process would only be defective with correct data. She discovered the value of carefully double-checking each input and transaction to guarantee its correctness and dependability.

The second principal Sarah discovered was organization, an essential quality in the bookkeeping industry. She had to create effective procedures and systems for organizing and keeping financial data to keep correct records. She discovered the importance of establishing guidelines for keeping track of invoices, receipts, and other vital paperwork and developing distinct, unambiguous categories for income and expenses.

Sarah learned the value of paying close attention to details as she learned more about bookkeeping. She soon saw how vital accuracy and dedication were in an area where even the slightest mistake might have far-reaching effects.

She developed a sharp eye for identifying irregularities and errors in financial records and made it a practice to review her work to ensure accuracy carefully.

However, Integrity may be the most significant lesson Sarah has taken away from her bookkeeping journey. She understood that, as a bookkeeper, she was entrusted with a position of trust and had a fiduciary duty to uphold the highest moral standards for her clients and employers. She was taught the value of honesty, openness, and secrecy and committed to following these values in her interactions, no matter what.

When Sarah reflected on her experience, she saw that the fundamentals of bookkeeping were a road map for success in the financial industry rather than merely a collection of ideas. Her firm grasp of accuracy, organization, detail-oriented Ness, and Integrity gave her confidence that she had all she needed to launch a lucrative career in accounting and beyond.

Equipped with this fresh understanding, Sarah boldly ventured into the world, keen to put her abilities to use and leave her imprint on the financial scene. She understood that she could accomplish anything she set her mind to after establishing the fundamentals of bookkeeping.

1.1 Clarifying Bookkeeping:

Its Nature and Importance

Amidst the bewildering array of numbers and the clamor of transactions in the maze-like world of finance, there is a quiet but vital art form called accounting. Many people associate "bookkeeping" with mysterious, intricate, old-fashioned accounting procedures and dusty ledgers. However, bookkeeping is more than a routine task—it is the backbone of financial management and the basis for all commercial dealings.

Documenting, arranging, and overseeing financial transactions inside an organization is the fundamental component of bookkeeping. Every financial transaction, whether small or large, leaves its stamp on the books, giving an accurate and transparent account of the money coming into and leaving the company.

You might wonder why bookkeeping is essential. Why is it crucial to financial management, and why should accountants and prospective business owners note it? The answer is found in the critical function that bookkeeping performs in the day-to-day operations of all businesses, big or small.

Fundamentally, bookkeeping offers a precise and transparent picture of a company's financial standing. Bookkeepers build a trail of breadcrumbs by carefully documenting each transaction in the firm. This trail helps managers and owners of the company monitor revenue and expenses, spot trends and patterns, and make well-informed decisions regarding the company's future course.

However, bookkeeping is more than just a tool for monitoring financial performance; it is also required by law and regulation for companies of all kinds. Businesses must keep accurate and current financial records for a specified amount of time in many jurisdictions as required by law; failing to do so may result in penalties, fines, and even legal action. By guaranteeing adherence to these rules, bookkeeping assures firms that they conduct their operations by the law.

Also, bookkeeping is necessary for tax compliance, especially for entrepreneurs and small business owners. Businesses may guarantee they pay the correct taxes yearly and prevent expensive penalties and audits from tax authorities by keeping precise records of their income and expenses. Additionally, bookkeeping helps businesses optimize their tax savings and minimize their tax liabilities by giving them essential data to justify tax deductions and credits.

However, bookkeeping's ability to support well-informed decision-making may be the most convincing argument for why it matters. Making informed decisions based on data can make all the difference in today's fast-paced business climate, where there are narrow margins and fierce rivalry. Bookkeeping gives businesses the timely and precise financial data they need to make well-informed decisions about everything from marketing campaigns and pricing strategies to potential investments and growth plans.

For instance, think of a tiny retail company that needs help making a profit. The company's owner finds out through examining its financial records that their overhead expenses are more significant than projected, reducing its profit margins. Equipped with this knowledge, businesses may pinpoint areas where they can reduce costs and boost productivity, eventually resulting in higher profitability and long-term success.

Or consider the situation of a startup business debating whether to go for outside funding to support its expansion. Potential investors can be assured of the company's business strategy and dedication to accountability and transparency by seeing clear and accurate financial statements backed up by thorough bookkeeping records. Consequently, this raises the possibility that it will obtain the capital required to grow its company.

These and innumerable other instances demonstrate how vital bookkeeping is for success in the corporate sector. It ensures that the law and regulations are followed. It facilitates informed decision-making at every company level and gives organizations the insights and information they need to prosper in today's competitive economy.

However, despite its significance, bookkeeping is still a part of financial management that needs to be understood. Addressed small company owners and entrepreneurs, it's an annoying task that must be avoided at all costs. However, as Sarah found out on her journey, bookkeeping is much more than a routine duty; it is a tremendous instrument for revealing a company's hidden potential, regardless of size.

In the following chapters, we will go deeper into bookkeeping and examine its complexities, learning the keys to creating a profitable home-based bookkeeping business and grasping the fundamentals of financial management. We will only stop once we achieve entrepreneurial perfection, from grasping the fundamentals of bookkeeping to negotiating the intricacies of tax compliance and financial reporting.

So come along with us, reader, as we set off on this exciting journey into the heart of the Bookkeeping Goldmine, where those brave enough to search them out will discover the secrets of financial prosperity. Together, we will solve the puzzles of bookkeeping and reveal its hidden benefits, creating a successful and fulfilling career path.

1.2 Crucial Knowledge and Requirements for Future Bookkeepers

A young woman named Emily lived in the vibrant city of Caryville, where skyscrapers stretched for the stars and the streets hummed with the energy of a million dreams. Emily had an ambitious heart and a passion for statistics, making her a visionary with big dreams. She had always been drawn to the financial industry and found comfort in the elegant simplicity of financial statements and mathematical computations.

Emily's love of numbers only grew as she got older. She read books on accounting and money cover to cover, taking in every pearl of knowledge they offered. She was sure that she would devote herself to the honorable bookkeeping profession when it came time to make her plans.

However, Emily quickly learned that bookkeeping involved much more than adding up and subtracting from ledgers.

It was a multidimensional field that called for a wide range of credentials and abilities necessary for any prospective bookkeeper to succeed. So, driven by a desire to grow and a thirst for information, Emily embarked on a mission to identify the prerequisite knowledge and abilities that would put her on the route to greatness.

Emily immediately learned how to pay attention to detail, which was a valuable talent in the bookkeeping industry. She soon saw how vital accuracy and dedication were in an area where even the slightest mistake might have far-reaching effects. She developed a sharp eye for identifying irregularities and errors in financial records and made it a practice to review her work to ensure accuracy carefully.

However, paying close attention to details was only the beginning. Emily quickly discovered that in addition to extraordinary analytical abilities, bookkeeping also required the capacity to comprehend financial facts and draw insightful conclusions.

She had to spot trends, patterns, and outliers while examining cash flow, income, and balance sheets to make judgments that would help her customers make financial decisions.

Emily learned the value of organization, analytical abilities, and attention to detail. She needed this quality to handle the piles of paper documents and digital files that accumulated daily on her desk. She discovered the value of establishing precise, well-defined procedures and systems for organizing and preserving financial data and putting tools and technology in place to improve productivity.

However, communication is arguably the most significant ability Emily discovered. She understood that as a bookkeeper, she would have to collaborate closely with her clients to comprehend their financial goals and objectives and effectively and succinctly explain intricate financial concepts.

She needed to speak clearly and establish rapport and trust with her clients, whether she was delivering financial reports to business owners or outlining tax laws to specific individuals.

As she continued her journey, Emily learned the value of lifelong learning and professional growth. She saw that to be competitive and give her clients the best possible service; she would need to stay up to date on the newest trends, technology, and laws in a business as dynamic and ever-changing as bookkeeping. She committed to continual learning, which would benefit her throughout her career, and looked for chances for continued education and training, whether through professional certifications, networking events, or online courses.

Perhaps Emily's most significant discovery was her strong desire to serve people. As a bookkeeper, she understood that she would be essential to her client's financial prosperity by assisting them in reaching their objectives and making wise judgments.

Whether guiding a small business owner through the intricacies of tax compliance or offering financial planning and budgeting assistance to an individual client, she was aware that her work had the potential to impact people's lives significantly.

As Emily reflected on her experience, she saw that the prerequisite knowledge and credentials for prospective bookkeepers were more than just a list of requirements; they were a path to success in the financial industry. She realized she had what it took to have a successful career in bookkeeping and beyond analytical skills, organization, communication, attention to detail, and a desire to serve people.

With a heart full of ambition and this newfound knowledge, Emily stepped out into the world with confidence, ready to put her skills to use and leave her mark on the financial scene. She understood that she could accomplish anything as long as she had the fundamental abilities and credentials of a bookkeeper.

1.3 Managing Law and Regulation Needs

A complex system of laws and regulations exists in the vast world of business, where the waves of trade come and go like the ocean's tides to regulate business conduct and safeguard the interests of consumers. Building a profitable home-based bookkeeping firm requires ambitious bookkeepers like Sarah to navigate this legal and regulatory environment successfully.

Fundamentally, the legal and regulatory structure that oversees the bookkeeping industry is intended to guarantee financial transactions are fair, transparent, and accountable. Aspiring bookkeepers need to be aware of a wide range of legal and regulatory requirements to run their businesses morally and legally, from tax and accounting standards to data protection and business license requirements.

Business license and registration are among the first legal and regulatory hurdles aspiring bookkeepers must overcome. Those who charge for bookkeeping services must either register their business with the relevant regulatory body or obtain a business license in many areas. Usually, this process includes filling up an application, paying a charge, and supplying credentials and professional liability insurance.

Getting a company license and registration are also necessary. Their company, prospective bookkeepers, must educate themselves on the tax laws and rules that apply to their industry. This entails knowing what is required to file income tax returns, collect and remit sales tax, and fulfil payroll tax obligations. It is crucial for bookkeepers to stay up to date on changes to tax rules and regulations and to obtain professional guidance when needed because noncompliance can result in expensive penalties and fines.

Comprehending data protection regulations is crucial in managing legal and regulatory obligations for bookkeepers. In light of the widespread adoption of cloud-based accounting software and the expansion of digital technology, bookkeepers need to take precautions to guarantee the privacy and security of their client's financial data. This could entail putting encryption and access controls in place, conducting frequent security assessments, and adhering to data protection regulations like the US's California Consumer Privacy Act (CCPA) and the EU's General Data Protection Regulation (GDPR).

Aspiring bookkeepers should know professional ethics, a code of behavior, tax laws, accounting standards, and data protection rules. These rules serve as a benchmark for moral decision-making in the workplace by outlining the values and expectations of behavior that regulate the behavior of bookkeepers and other financial professionals.

Bookkeepers can show their dedication to maintaining the highest standards of professionalism and Integrity by abiding by these codes of conduct and ethics, which will also help them gain the respect and credibility of their clients and colleagues.

However, managing risk and shielding oneself and one's clients from potential legal responsibilities are just as important as complying with legal and regulatory requirements for bookkeepers. This could entail creating solid contractual agreements with clients that specify the scope of services and responsibilities, getting professional liability insurance to guard against claims of carelessness or errors and omissions, and getting legal counsel when needed to handle complicated legal issues or disputes.

Aspiring bookkeepers need to take preventative steps and be ready to react to legal and regulatory issues as they arise. Bookkeepers must be prepared to handle situations involving tax authorities, disgruntled clients, and data breaches exposing confidential financial information with professionalism and Integrity.

They should consult legal experts for advice and take necessary steps to minimize risks and safeguard their clients and interests.

Though managing legal and regulatory requirements as a bookkeeper can be complicated, Sarah was sure she could overcome any obstacle and establish a profitable home-based bookkeeping firm with the correct information, abilities, and assistance. Equipped with an extensive comprehension of tax laws and regulations, data protection regulations, professional codes of conduct and ethics, risk management strategies, and business licensing and registration, she felt secure in maneuvering through the legal and regulatory maze and establishing a long-lasting, profitable enterprise.

So, driven by a strong sense of purpose and resolve, Sarah embarked on her journey, eager to leave her mark on the bookkeeping industry and create a company that would uphold the highest standards of professionalism, Integrity, and ethical behavior besides attending to her client's requirements because she was aware that success in the intricate and dynamic world of finance depended not only on complex data but also on an awareness of and ability to navigate the legal and regulatory framework that governs company activity.

Chapter 2:

Setting Up Your Home Office

A home office is a haven of work and creativity in the middle of suburban peace, among the soft sounds of singing birds and rustling branches. For ambitious bookkeepers like Emily, establishing a home office is essential to building a profitable business, not only for convenience's sake.

Emily was excited and full of expectation as she took in the area that would soon become her home office. She knew that this was where her ambitions would come true and that she would go out on a quest for self-awareness and entrepreneurship. But as she looked around the space, it became clear that meticulous planning and attention to detail would be needed to turn it into a valuable and inspirational workstation.

Emily recognized that creating a designated workspace free from interruptions and distractions was the first step in organizing her home office. For Emily, this meant dividing off a section of her living room and furnishing it with a strong desk, a cozy chair, and enough shelving for her office supplies, files, and books.

However, setting up a specific workstation was only the first step. Emily also knew that she would need to create an inspiring and stimulating environment in her home office to optimize her output and creativity.

This meant surrounding herself with things that made her happy and inspired her, whether it was a warm rug to keep her feet toasty on winter mornings, a motivational statement to keep her focused on her objectives, or a potted plant to provide a little greenery.

Emily became increasingly aware of the significance of ergonomics—a crucial but frequently disregarded component of workspace design—as she dug further into assembling her home office. Having spent many hours at her workplace, she knew purchasing an adjustable desk and ergonomic chair would be crucial to preserving her long-term health and wellbeing. She kept her keyboard and mouse within easy reach and angled her computer monitor at eye level to reduce strain on her neck, shoulders, and wrists.

However, designing an environment that encouraged focus and concentration was just as important when setting up a home office as it was about comfort. Emily knew that to do this, she would have to reduce outside distractions and establish a clear boundary between her Personal and professional lives. This required her to set up unambiguous family boundaries, designate particular hours for work and play, and put mechanisms in place to deal with everyday distractions like social media, email, and housework.

Emily made sure her home office had all the tools and technology she would need to be successful, in addition to designing it for optimal comfort and efficiency. This required making purchases of a dependable computer, a fast internet connection, and software and apps that would help her keep productive and organized. Emily ensured her home office had all the tools she needed to run her firm efficiently, from project management to accounting software.

Making her home office feel like hers, a place that embodied her values and personality, was the most crucial part of setting it up. Emily made sure that her home office reflected who she was and what she stood for, whether it was by adding her favorite colors and textures into the décor, hanging artwork on the walls, or placing family photos on her desk.

Emily felt a wave of pleasure and accomplishment sweep over her as she finished her home office and stood back to appreciate her work. She realized that this was more than simply a place to work; it was a safe refuge where she could follow her passions and realize her aspirations. And she knew that there was no limit to what she could do when she sat down at her desk, ready to start her entrepreneurial path, with her home office serving as her anchor.

2.1 Creating an Ergonomic and Productive Workspace

A well-designed workspace is essential to any successful business, whether a home office or a busy corporate headquarters. It is a haven of productivity and creativity where goals are realized and dreams come true. For ambitious bookkeepers like Sarah, creating a functional and aesthetically pleasing workstation is essential to setting the groundwork for future success.

Sarah recognized that every detail, down to the arrangement of her computer display, would significantly impact her overall wellbeing and productivity when she set out to design the ideal workstation. In light of this, she created a workstation to encourage proper posture, lessen the chance of pain and injury, and excite and invigorate her.

Sarah knew selecting an appropriate location was the first step towards creating an ergonomic and productive workstation. For Sarah, this meant locating a peaceful area in her house where she could concentrate on her work without being bothered or distracted. She thought about it and decided on a spare room that seemed like her haven because it had lots of natural light and a serene atmosphere.

After deciding on the ideal spot, Sarah focused on organizing her workstation. She knew she needed to arrange her workspace to reduce clutter and increase usefulness to improve her output and efficiency. To achieve this, she invested in a substantial desk that offered a generous amount of surface area for arranging her work and sufficient storage for her books, files, and office supplies.

However, creating an atmosphere that encouraged focus and concentration was just as important as building an aesthetically pleasing workstation. To do this, Sarah arranged her workplace to limit outside distractions and maximize natural light, which helped her stay focused and motivated all day. To add a feeling of peace and tranquility, she added natural elements to her desk, such as little fountains and potted plants.

Sarah considered ergonomics as she dug further into creating her workspace—a crucial but frequently disregarded component of workspace design. Having spent many hours at her workplace, she knew purchasing an adjustable desk and ergonomic chair would preserve her long-term health and wellbeing. She kept her keyboard and mouse within easy reach to reduce strain on her neck, shoulders, and wrists and angled her computer monitor at eye level.

However, building a workspace that was both ergonomic and productive required more than simply considering physical comfort; it also needed to consider Sarah's values and personality. Sarah ensured that her workstation reflected her values and identity by adding her favorite colors and textures to the décor, hanging artwork on the walls, or placing pictures of her loved ones on her desk.

Sarah felt a wave of joy and achievement sweep over her as she finished her workspace and stood back to appreciate her work. She realized that this was more than simply a place to work; it was her haven where she could follow her dreams and fulfil her ambitions. She felt there was no limit to what she could do when she sat down at her desk, ready to start her entrepreneurial path, with her efficient and well-designed workspace serving as her fulcrum.

2.2 Choosing the Appropriate Hardware and Software

The correct hardware and software selection is crucial for building a productive and effective workspace in the digital age, where technology is king and creativity is unrestricted. Selecting the appropriate tools of the trade can determine whether someone succeeds or fails ambitious bookkeepers like Emily in the cutthroat business world.

Emily realized that every choice she made, from the kind of computer she used to the accounting software she relied on, would significantly impact her workflow and productivity as she set out to choose the proper tools and software for her home office. In light of this, she decided to investigate and assess the several choices at her disposal, analyzing each option's advantages and disadvantages closely to ensure that her choices would position her for success.

Emily started by thinking about her computer, which would serve as the main instrument for her bookkeeping firm and the foundation of her home office. After considering it, she decided to spend money on a powerful laptop to provide her and her clients with smooth communication and collaboration. It also needed a dependable internet connection and plenty of processing and storage capability.

However, choosing the ideal computer was only the first step. To complete her setup, Emily also needed to select the appropriate peripherals and accessories, such as a cozy keyboard and mouse, a high-resolution monitor for a clear and sharp display, and a good printer/scanner for generating and sharing documents. She made sure to spend money on ergonomic add-ons, such as a wrist rest for the keyboard and a monitor stand that could be adjusted to encourage proper posture and lower the chance of pain and harm.

To support her bookkeeping firm, Emily needed to choose the appropriate software tools in addition to hardware. This includes project management software to keep track of her assignments and due dates, accounting software to handle her clients' financial records, and communication tools to maintain relationships with her clients and coworkers. Emily decided to invest in a cloud-based accounting software that provided extensive functionality, an easy-to-use interface, and interfaces with other company products and services after investigating her options and reading evaluations from other industry experts.

However, choosing the best software requires consideration of compatibility, scalability, and usefulness. Emily knew that her software tools would need to change and adapt as her firm did to meet her ever-changing needs and advancing capabilities. In light of this, she selected software programs that had scalable functionality and adjustable price structures, enabling her to upgrade or downgrade as needed without incurring extra fees or interfering with her workflow.

While Emily persisted in investigating and assessing her choices, she also asked coworkers, mentors, and industry experts for suggestions and advice. She inquired about demos and trials from vendors to experience their products directly and participated in webinars and workshops on software selection and deployment. With an abundance of information and understanding, Emily was able to make wise choices that would position her for success in her accounting company.

However, picking the appropriate hardware and software required more than just deciding on the newest and most potent instruments; it also required her to be aware of her requirements and preferences as a bookkeeper. Since every bookkeeper has a different workflow and set of needs, Emily wanted to ensure the tools she chose would help her achieve her particular goals and objectives. Whether it was a task management app with a basic design or accounting software with a ton of features, Emily made sure to select tools that would improve rather than hinder her workflow and productivity.

Emily experienced excitement and anticipation as she finished her home office and turned on her new computer for the first time. She knew this was the start of a new chapter in her career as a bookkeeper, full of opportunity and promise and supported at every turn by the appropriate tools and software. Knowing that she could accomplish anything as long as she had the necessary tools, she sat at her desk, prepared to start her entrepreneurial journey.

2.3 Setting Up Effective Processes and Mechanisms

It takes precision and accuracy to record, analyze, and arrange every transaction in the fast-paced world of bookkeeping; therefore, creating effective workflows and systems is crucial to success. In addition to increasing productivity, streamlining procedures and systems guarantees consistency and dependability in the work of prospective bookkeepers like Sarah.

Sarah understood that meticulous preparation and attention to detail would benefit every facet of her business, from file management to client contact, as she set out to create effective workflows and procedures in her home office. In light of this, she developed procedures and frameworks to optimize effectiveness, reduce mistakes, and offer her clients and associates a flawless experience.

Sarah knew that outlining her bookkeeping business's many jobs and procedures was the first step towards creating effective workflows and systems. This included data input, financial analysis, reporting, and client onboarding. Sarah was able to analyze her process and pinpoint areas for improvement by dissecting each task into its constituent pieces, locating dependencies, and finding bottlenecks.

After mapping out her workflow, Sarah focused on making every stage of the procedure as efficient as possible. This required finding ways to automate routine processes, standardizing practices to guarantee dependability and consistency, and establishing safeguards and inspections to identify mistakes before they got out of hand. Sarah was able to save time and lower her risk of expensive errors by optimizing her workflow and getting rid of pointless procedures. This freed her up to concentrate on more high-value tasks that would expand her company.

However, creating effective processes and systems requires cooperation and communication in addition to automation. Sarah understood that she would need to keep lines of communication open and work well with her partners and colleagues to give her clients the best service possible. To achieve this, she established procedures for exchanging files and documents, setting up appointments and meetings, and monitoring assignments and due dates. This ensured that everyone engaged in the process was aware of their responsibilities and working toward the same objective.

Sarah understood the value of cooperation, communication, data protection, and privacy for her bookkeeping company. She understood the critical need to protect her client's data because sensitive financial information was at risk. She implemented stringent security measures to prevent unwanted access to or publication of her client's information, including encryption and access controls. Additionally, she kept up with the most recent cybersecurity dangers and vulnerabilities, taking preventative measures to lower risks and safeguard the interests of her clients.

However, ongoing improvement was likely crucial in setting up effective workflows and systems. Sarah knew that she would need to continuously assess and analyze her processes and systems to find chances for innovation and optimization if she wanted to remain competitive in the quick-paced field of bookkeeping. Sarah was dedicated to constant learning and development because she understood that it was essential for her company's long-term success, whether by implementing new software tools to expedite her operations or honing her communication techniques to serve her clients better.

Sarah was happy as she completed her workflows and systems and took a moment to appreciate her efforts. She understood this was more than simply a set of guidelines and protocols; it was the cornerstone of her bookkeeping company and the basis for her future success. She knew there was no limit to what she could do when she sat down at her desk, ready to start her entrepreneurial journey with effective workflows and procedures in place.

Chapter 3:

Establishing Your Brand

In the dynamic and competitive business world, where companies strive to stand out, and customers search for the perfect solutions, establishing a powerful and unforgettable brand is crucial for achieving prosperity. For Emily, a bookkeeper looking to develop her brand, creating a logo or a catchy slogan is just the beginning. She understands the importance of crafting a distinct identity that connects with her clients and helps her stand out in a crowded market.

Emily understood the importance of every detail in her business, recognizing that her logo, website, marketing materials, and client interactions would all contribute to how her brand was perceived and its reputation. Approaching the task with the precision of a market research analyst, she embarked on the mission to establish a brand that would embody her core principles, effectively convey her knowledge, and instill a sense of reliability and assurance in her clientele.

Emily understood that establishing her brand required clearly defining her identity. This would encompass her role as a bookkeeper and the values she represented as a business. She had to carefully analyze her target audience, gaining deep insights into their desires and preferences. Additionally, she had to communicate her distinct value proposition and establish a strong position in the competitive market. With a keen understanding of her target audience, Emily crafted a distinct brand identity that effectively communicated her unique value proposition. This enabled her to captivate her ideal clients and give them an edge in the market.

Emily focused on developing visual elements to give her brand a vibrant and engaging presence. As a market research analyst, I crafted a logo that perfectly encapsulated her brand's essence and effectively conveyed her professionalism and expertise. Additionally, I meticulously chose colors, fonts, and imagery that harmonized with her brand's unique personality and core values.

With a well-crafted brand identity, Emily made her mark in the marketplace, ensuring that clients easily recognize and remember her brand.

However, establishing a brand went beyond just appearances; it also involved forging significant relationships with her clients and community. Emily prioritized establishing strong connections and cultivating trust and credibility in her interactions with clients and colleagues. Emily consistently demonstrated her brand's values in all aspects of her work, from delivering exceptional customer service to producing high-quality results. Her commitment to giving back to her community through volunteering and philanthropy further solidified her reputation, earning her clients' and peers' loyalty and respect.

Emily understood the significance of cultivating a robust online presence for her brand while fostering connections. Understanding the importance of a well-designed and user-friendly website, Emily recognized the need to cater to the growing number of consumers who rely on the internet for product and service research.

She strategically invested in a professionally designed website that showcased her services and expertise. The website also offered valuable resources and content tailored to her target audience. Emily successfully positioned herself as a trusted authority by creating an informative and engaging website. As a result, she attracted clients who were enthusiastic about collaborating with her.

However, establishing a brand relied not only on Emily's words but also on the opinions of others. Emily prioritized establishing her reputation and credibility by collecting testimonials and reviews from contented clients. She advised her clients to share their feedback on her website and social media platforms, as well as on popular review sites such as Yelp and Google My Business. By highlighting the favorable experiences of her clients, Emily successfully established social proof and credibility, which enhanced the trust and brand preference of potential clients.

Emily actively sought networking and collaboration opportunities with professionals in her industry as she worked on building her brand and expanding her reach. Emily actively sought opportunities to connect with individuals who shared similar interests and expertise through networking events and industry conferences, joining professional associations and groups, and engaging in online forums and communities. Through establishing connections with fellow professionals, Emily broadened her network, acquired valuable insights and guidance, and remained up-to-date with the industry's latest trends and advancements.

Remaining authentic and staying true to her values were crucial in building her brand. Emily understood the importance of establishing a brand that genuinely connected with her clients and community. She recognized the need to be sincere and authentic in her interactions and communications.

Emily consistently stayed true to herself and her brand's values, whether by sharing her story and journey as a bookkeeper, expressing her passion for helping others achieve their financial goals, or standing up for causes she believed in. She understood authenticity was crucial in building lasting connections and loyalty with her audience.

Emily felt pride and accomplishment as she reflected on her journey to build her brand. She understood this went beyond a logo or website; it represented her tireless effort, unwavering commitment, and deep love for her work. With her sharp observation skills and understanding of market trends and consumer behavior, she envisioned a limitless future for her bookkeeping business, built upon a solid and unforgettable brand.

3.1 Developing Your Unique Selling Proposition

Amidst the crowded marketplace, where businesses constantly compete for attention, creating a distinct selling point is like unfurling a vibrant sail among a fleet of ships. It is a valuable tool, providing insights and direction to attract customers to your business. Aspiring bookkeepers like Sarah understand the importance of creating a strong Unique Selling Proposition (USP). It goes beyond simply standing out from the competition. It's about effectively communicating the distinct value she offers to her clients and positioning herself as the trusted authority in her industry.

With the mindset of a market research analyst, Sarah delved into the task of defining her unique selling proposition. She understood the importance of thoroughly examining her strengths to discover what distinguished her from other bookkeepers.

With the mindset of a market research analyst, she understood the importance of going beyond just providing top-notch bookkeeping services. She recognized the need to pinpoint her strengths, talents, and attributes that would connect with her target clients and convince them to select her over her rivals.

Understanding the target audience's needs and desires is crucial for Sarah as she crafts her unique selling proposition (USP). Who were the clients that she specifically targeted? What were the difficulties they encountered in their businesses? What were they looking for in terms of solutions? With a deep understanding of her target audience and a keen ability to connect with their needs, Sarah gained valuable insights that shaped her unique selling proposition and allowed her to craft a message that truly resonated with her audience.

Adopting the mindset of a market research analyst, Sarah meticulously analyzed her target audience to gain a deep understanding. She then focused on pinpointing her distinct strengths and capabilities as a bookkeeper. What made her stand out from other bookkeepers in terms of her skills? What experiences and qualifications did she possess? With a keen eye for analysis, Sarah meticulously evaluated her abilities and reflected on her achievements. This allowed her to identify her distinct strengths and utilize them strategically.

Sarah deeply understood a particular niche in the bookkeeping industry, which set her apart. Unlike other bookkeepers, Sarah has focused on assisting small businesses in the creative industry. With a keen grasp of the financial requirements of artists, writers, and designers, she was dedicated to supporting their growth and success.

Sarah's dedication to outstanding customer service and cultivating robust client relationships set her apart. Like a market research analyst, Sarah went beyond the typical bookkeeper role by deeply understanding her client's businesses and goals. She provided personalized advice and support to ensure their success. She demonstrated exceptional dedication to ensuring her client's satisfaction, which resulted in earning their trust and loyalty.

With her keen understanding and careful evaluation, Sarah embarked on the task of creating her USP. This concise and captivating statement effectively conveyed the distinct value she offered to her clients, setting her apart from her rivals. After careful consideration and multiple rounds of refinement, she ultimately decided on the following unique selling proposition:

"With my extensive experience providing financial services to small businesses in the creative industry, I provide customized financial solutions designed to meet your individual needs and objectives. I promise to give you great customer service. And making sure you ensuring clearly understand your finances, allowing you to concentrate on your core strengths—your creative endeavors."

Sarah's unique strengths, talents, and attributes were effectively captured in her USP, which directly addressed the needs and desires of her target audience. It conveyed her expertise in catering to small businesses in the creative industry, her unwavering focus on providing personalized service, and her unwavering determination to assist her clients in achieving success. Her statement was impactful, distinguishing her from other bookkeepers and establishing her as the perfect option for creative entrepreneurs needing skilled financial advice.

Like a market research analyst, Sarah's journey to build her brand and attract clients to her business began with crafting her unique selling proposition (USP). Approaching her task with the precision of a market research analyst, she crafted a well-rounded marketing strategy. Her goal was clear: to connect with her desired audience and convey her distinct value proposition with utmost clarity.

She is creating a captivating brand story highlighting her dedication to assisting small businesses in the creative industry and crafting an aesthetically pleasing brand identity that mirrors her character and principles. She also focused on building a robust online presence by creating a website, managing social media profiles, and maintaining a blog. These platforms allowed her to share valuable content and connect meaningfully with her audience.

One key element of Sarah's marketing strategy was ensuring that her unique selling proposition (USP) was effectively communicated across all channels. This included maintaining a consistent and genuine message across her website, email newsletters, and client interactions. With a keen understanding of her unique selling proposition and a strategic approach to positioning herself as an industry expert, Sarah successfully attracted clients who shared her values and were enthusiastic about collaborating with her.

As Sarah thought about her journey to develop her unique selling proposition, she couldn't help but feel a surge of satisfaction and anticipation. She understood that this went beyond a mere marketing slogan. It was the core of her brand, defining her identity as a bookkeeper and business owner. With a clear vision for the future, she was confident that her unique selling proposition would lead her to great success in her bookkeeping business.

3.2 Creating an Engaging Brand Identity

In the dynamic business world, where numerous brands vie for consumers' attention and loyalty, establishing a captivating brand identity is crucial for differentiating yourself and fostering a meaningful bond with your audience. For Emily, a bookkeeper looking to develop her brand, the process goes beyond designing a logo or creating a memorable tagline. It involves conveying her personality, values, and unique selling points to potential clients, setting her apart from competitors.

Emily understood the importance of every aspect of her brand identity, recognizing that her logo, color palette, tone of voice, and customer experience would all contribute to how her audience perceived her brand. Approaching the task with the mindset of a market research analyst, she embarked on the mission of crafting a brand identity that would not only captivate the eyes but also resonate with authenticity, leave a lasting impression, and genuinely embody her core values and unique personality.

Emily understood that to establish her brand identity, she must clearly define her brand's personality and values. These unique traits and characteristics would help her stand out from her competitors and connect with her desired audience.

Did her brand have a playful and whimsical vibe, or did it lean more toward professionalism and authority? Did it showcase a forward-thinking and pioneering approach, or did it embody a more conventional and proven methodology? By answering these questions and pinpointing her brand's fundamental values and personality traits, Emily established the groundwork for her brand identity and directed her creative choices for the future.

Emily focused on developing visual elements that effectively represent her brand's personality and values. As a market research analyst, I crafted a logo that perfectly encapsulated her brand's essence and effectively conveyed her professionalism and expertise.

Additionally, I meticulously chose colors, fonts, and imagery that harmonized with her brand's unique personality and core values. With a well-crafted and visually captivating brand identity, Emily successfully established a powerful and unforgettable presence in the market. This made it effortless for clients to identify and recall her brand.

Ensuring a seamless and unified brand experience across all contact points was crucial in developing a compelling brand identity. It went beyond just aesthetics. Emily meticulously curated her online presence, ensuring that every aspect of her brand, from her website and social media profiles to her business cards and marketing materials, exuded her core values and distinctive persona.

She effectively conveyed her unique selling proposition to her target audience through these touchpoints. She created a unified brand experience that resonated with her audience and reinforced her brand's identity using consistent messaging, imagery, and design elements.

Emily dedicated her efforts to crafting her brand's tone of voice, ensuring that her communication style resonated with her audience. Did her brand have a casual and conversational tone, or was it more formal and professional? Did it have a witty tone, or was it more straightforward and informative? With a keen understanding of her brand's target audience, Emily strategically crafted her messaging and communications to establish a unique and memorable brand personality. This approach allowed her to connect with her audience deeper and stand out from her competitors.

Ensuring authenticity and staying true to herself were crucial to developing her brand identity. Emily understood the importance of establishing an authentic and open connection with her audience to create a brand that genuinely connected with them. Emily consistently stayed true to herself and her brand's values, whether by sharing her story and journey as a bookkeeper, expressing her passion for helping others achieve their financial goals, or standing up for causes she believed in.

She understood authenticity was crucial in building lasting connections and loyalty with her audience.

Emily felt pride and satisfaction reflecting on her journey to develop her brand identity. She understood that this went beyond a mere logo or color scheme. It represented her identity as a bookkeeper and business owner, encapsulated in a visual and verbal form that deeply connected with her audience. With a clear vision of the future, she recognized that her strong brand identity would be the key to unlocking endless possibilities in her bookkeeping business.

3.3 Marketing Strategies to Attract Clients

Successful marketing is crucial for attracting clients and expanding your brand in the fast-paced business realm, where competition is intense and consumer attention is fleeting. For Sarah, an aspiring bookkeeper, crafting a well-rounded marketing strategy goes beyond simply advertising her services. It involves building genuine relationships with her desired audience and positioning herself as a reliable expert in her industry.

Like a savvy marketer, Sarah soon discovered many strategies and tactics to attract clients to her bookkeeping business effectively. Equipped with diverse tactics, the options seemed limitless, spanning from traditional networking and word-of-mouth referrals to cutting-edge techniques like social media marketing and content creation. As Sarah considered her options, she recognized the importance of choosing strategies that powerfully connect with her target audience and reflect her brand's values and objectives.

Networking was a successful marketing strategy for Sarah as she focused on establishing connections with professionals in her industry and local community. This approach allowed her to cultivate referrals and leads, benefiting her business. Sarah actively sought opportunities to connect with individuals who shared similar interests and expertise through networking events and industry conferences, joining professional associations and Joining groups, or engaging in online forums and communities. Through establishing connections with fellow professionals, Sarah broadened her network, acquired valuable insights and advice, and accessed fresh prospects for growth and collaboration.

Alongside networking, Sarah effectively employed content marketing to attract clients to her business. Through creating valuable and informative content, Sarah effectively demonstrated her expertise and offered valuable resources to her target audience. With her expertise and knowledge, Sarah gave her audience valuable tips and advice on managing finances. She had a knack for explaining complex accounting, straightforwardly explaining ideas, and simplifying things for her readers. Additionally, Sarah shared her clients' success stories and case studies, further establishing her credibility and authority in her field.

One of the critical strengths of content marketing was its remarkable ability to draw in clients through search engines and social media naturally. Sarah kept an eye on market trends and consumer behavior; Sarah strategically tailored her content to align with the interests and needs of her target audience. As a result, her online visibility skyrocketed, attracting a consistent flow of potential clients actively interested in bookkeeping services. Like a market research analyst, Sarah strategically shared her content on popular social media platforms like Facebook, LinkedIn, and Twitter. This allowed her to expand her reach and connect with her followers more intimately, gradually establishing trust and credibility.

Sarah successfully utilized email marketing to connect with her audience, cultivate potential customers, and advertise her services. Sarah successfully cultivated an email list of engaged prospects and clients with a strategic approach. This allowed her to deliver personalized content and exclusive offers directly to their inboxes, ensuring her brand stayed at the forefront of their minds and fostering repeat business. By consistently sending out monthly newsletters filled with valuable tips and advice, announcing exclusive promotions and discounts, and sharing regular updates and news about her business, Sarah successfully maintained the interest and engagement of her audience through her email marketing efforts.

Consistency was a crucial element in Sarah's marketing strategy. With a keen understanding of the importance of brand awareness and client attraction, she recognized the need to establish a cohesive presence across various channels and touchpoints. This encompassed her website, social media profiles, email newsletters, and client interactions. With a deep understanding of her audience's needs and preferences, Sarah skillfully crafted content and messaging that consistently struck a chord. This unwavering commitment to providing value allowed her to establish trust and credibility, positioning herself as the trusted authority in her industry. As a result, she effortlessly attracted enthusiastic clients to collaborate with her.

As Sarah looked back on her marketing journey, a wave of pride and satisfaction washed over her. She understood this was more than a mere compilation of tactics and strategies. It represented her tireless effort, unwavering commitment, and sincere willingness to help others achieve their financial objectives. With a clear vision for the future, she was confident that her well-rounded marketing strategy would propel her bookkeeping business to great heights.

Chapter 4:

Becoming Proficient in Bookkeeping Fundamentals

In the world of business, where every transaction has its narrative and every dollar spent or earned has a lasting impact, having a solid grasp of bookkeeping fundamentals is like becoming fluent in the language of commerce. For individuals interested in bookkeeping, like Emily, gaining a solid understanding of these foundational principles goes beyond simply reconciling accounts. It involves comprehending a company's financial well-being, offering clients valuable perspectives, and establishing a solid foundation for achievement.

Emily discovered that bookkeeping is a complex field that goes beyond surface-level understanding. Just like a meticulous record-keeper, she delved into the principles of double-entry accounting and honed her skills in financial analysis. Countless concepts and techniques awaited her, demanding her dedication and excellence in her chosen field. With unwavering resolve and relentless effort, she embarked on a journey to master these essential skills and establish a strong base for her profession as a meticulous record keeper.

In bookkeeping, the foundation is built upon the principle of double-entry accounting. This method guarantees precision and uniformity when recording financial transactions in the books. Emily discovered the importance of maintaining balance in the books by ensuring that every transaction has a debit and a credit. Emily swiftly mastered applying double-entry accounting principles to preserve her client's financial records meticulously. She effortlessly records revenue from sales, expenses from purchases, and assets and liabilities from loans, ensuring everything is in perfect order.

Understanding the ins and outs of bookkeeping goes beyond simply recording transactions. It involves grasping the various types of accounts and their interconnectedness.

Emily learned about the three primary types of accounts: assets, liabilities, and Equity, along with the different subcategories within each. She became skilled at categorizing transactions into the correct accounts, guaranteeing that the books precisely portrayed her clients' businesses' financial standing.

Emily gained knowledge not only in recording transactions and managing accounts but also in understanding the significance of financial statements. These documents are crucial summaries of a business's economic performance and position. She mastered the art of preparing the three essential financial statements.

The income statement reveals the ins and outs of a business's revenues and expenses. The balance sheet provides a snapshot of Tracking details about a business's assets, debts, and ownership at a particular time. Lastly, the cash flow statement sheds light on cash flow in and out of a business's operations, investments, and financing activities.

However, the key to becoming proficient in bookkeeping was honing the ability to analyze financial data and offer valuable insights to clients. Emily gained the skills to thoroughly examine financial statements, evaluating the business's profitability, liquidity, and solvency. She also became adept at spotting trends and patterns that could impact its future performance. With this knowledge, she provided practical recommendations and strategic guidance to her clients, enabling them to make well-informed choices and reach their financial objectives.

Emily's journey into bookkeeping was filled with constant challenges and exciting opportunities for personal and professional development. She tackled the ins and outs of accrual accounting, bank reconciliations, and payroll processing with unwavering enthusiasm and determination. She understood that these fundamentals were crucial for her success as a bookkeeper.

However, the most fulfilling part of understanding bookkeeping fundamentals was witnessing her efforts' positive influence on her clients' businesses. Just like a meticulous record keeper, she guided them through their financial obstacles and helped them reach their aspirations. Emily's work as a bookkeeper had a profound impact on the world. She helped small business owners boost their profitability, supported nonprofit organizations in managing their funds, and guided startup entrepreneurs through financial planning. Her dedication to her role was evident in the positive changes she brought about.

As Emily looked back on her journey to become proficient in bookkeeping, she couldn't help but feel grateful for her opportunities and knowledge. She understood this was more than just a job—a deep-seated commitment, a burning desire to provide exceptional service to others. As she envisioned her future, she was confident that her firm grasp of bookkeeping fundamentals would pave the way for endless possibilities in her career.

4.1 Understanding Financial Statements: Balance Sheets, Income Statements, and Cash Flow Statements

Like a meticulous observer, financial statements combine the narrative of a company's economic well-being and achievements. For individuals interested in bookkeeping, a thorough understanding of crucial financial documents such as balance sheets, income statements, and cash flow statements goes beyond mere number-crunching. It involves interpreting the intricate language of finance and extracting valuable insights to inform decision-making and strategic planning.

A Glimpse into Financial Stability

Picture a still frame, capturing a singular moment in the existence of a business, unveiling its assets, liabilities, and Equity. Think of it as a snapshot of a company's financial position at a specific time, capturing the essence of a balance sheet. For Sarah, becoming an expert in the balance sheet felt like gaining insight into the inner workings of a business, comprehending its strengths, weaknesses, and overall financial well-being.

In the core of the balance sheet, we find the essential accounting equation: Assets = Liabilities + Equity. This equation is crucial for maintaining the balance sheet's balance, ensuring that every transaction recorded in the books is accurately accounted for. Assets are the valuable resources that a company owns or controls, including cash, inventory, and property. Conversely, liabilities indicate the company's obligations or debts, including loans, accounts payable, and accrued expenses. Equity signifies the shareholders' interest in the business, encompassing their capital investment, accumulated profits, and additional equity contributions.

As Sarah immersed herself in the world of balance sheets, she gained a deep understanding of how to analyze different elements and ratios to evaluate a company's financial well-being and stability. She became skilled at calculating essential ratios such as the current and debt-to-equity ratios, which gave her valuable insights into a company's liquidity and leverage. With this expertise, Sarah effortlessly analyzed trends and patterns in the balance sheet, quickly identifying potential issues and providing valuable recommendations to her clients to enhance their financial standing.

Income Statements: A Detailed Look at Revenue and Expenses.

Like a meticulous record-keeper, the balance sheet captures a moment in time. At the same time, the income statement tells a captivating story of a company's financial journey over a specific period. For Sarah, understanding the income statement was akin to deciphering a complex puzzle and assembling a company's financial performance, costs, and overall profitability narrative.

The income statement concisely overviews a company's earnings and expenditures during a designated timeframe, a month, quarter, or year. It starts with the company's revenues, which are the earnings from sales of goods or services. Then, it deducts the expenses associated with generating those revenues. This calculation gives us the net income or loss for the period. Understanding the income statement is crucial for stakeholders to assess a company's profitability, efficiency, and growth potential.

It provides valuable insights into the company's performance and highlights areas for improvement.

As Sarah meticulously examined income statements, she gained valuable insights into dissecting the different elements and ratios to evaluate a company's financial performance and profitability. She became proficient in calculating essential metrics. Calculating the gross, operating, and net profit margins is critical for analyzing financial performance, giving her valuable insights into the company's efficiency and profitability. With a keen eye for detail, Sarah meticulously analyzed the income statement, uncovering both areas of strength and weakness. She skillfully identified opportunities for cost savings and revenue growth, enabling her to provide valuable strategic recommendations to her clients. Her expertise helped her clients improve their bottom line and achieve tremendous success.

Cash flow statements are essential for the smooth operation of any business.

Although the balance sheet and income statement offer valuable insights into a company's financial position and performance, they only provide a partial picture. To understand a company's economic well-being comprehensively, Sarah recognized the importance of familiarizing herself with the cash flow statement, a crucial financial analysis component.

The cash flow statement records the cash coming in and going out of a company's operations, investments, and financing activities during a designated time frame. It offers valuable information on generating and utilizing cash within the business, aiding stakeholders in comprehending the company's liquidity, solvency, and capacity to fulfil its financial responsibilities. Through careful analysis of the cash flow statement, Sarah gained valuable insights into the company's financial patterns and trends. This allowed her to assess the company's cash generation capabilities from its core operations and make informed decisions regarding investments and debt management.

As Sarah immersed herself in the world of cash flow statements, she gained a deep understanding of how to analyze and interpret the different sections and categories to evaluate a company's cash flow patterns. She became skilled at calculating important metrics like cash flow for spending, financing, and running the business, which gave her valuable insights into how cash was generated and used. With this knowledge, Sarah could spot potential cash flow issues or opportunities, devise strategies to enhance cash flow management, and provide valuable guidance to her clients to maximize their financial performance.

Integration and Interpretation: Making Connections

As Sarah delved into financial statements, she understood that every statement conveyed a distinct narrative about a company's fiscal well-being and achievements.

Like a meticulous record keeper, the balance sheet captures a precise moment in the company's financial journey. At the same time, the income statement sheds light on its ability to generate profits and operate efficiently over time. Meanwhile, the cash flow statement provides valuable insights into the company's cash flow patterns and overall liquidity.

However, more than comprehending each statement individually needed to be improved; Sarah recognized that true expertise came from combining and analyzing the information from all three statements. With a keen eye for detail and a systematic approach, Sarah was able to piece together the puzzle of a company's financial situation Through a careful analysis of the balance sheet, income statement, and cash flow statement. This allowed her to uncover hidden trends and ideas that might not be clear at first from any statement alone.

With a keen eye for detail and a deep understanding of her client's financial needs, Sarah offered valuable insights and recommendations to guide them through their financial challenges and help them reach their goals. With her keen sense of financial statements, Sarah has provided invaluable guidance to small business owners, startup entrepreneurs, and nonprofit organizations. Her expertise has helped her clients improve profitability, manage cash flow, and navigate financial planning and budgeting.

As Sarah reflected on her journey to become proficient in bookkeeping, she felt a deep sense of accomplishment and fulfilment. She knew that her newfound expertise would have a meaningful impact on her clients' lives. She deeply understood the intricacies of numbers, but it went beyond that. It was about unravelling the tales woven within financial statements, speaking the language of business fluently, and harnessing that knowledge to bring about meaningful transformations and leave a lasting mark.

With her expertise in financial statement analysis, she had complete confidence in her ability to excel in her career as a bookkeeper and reach new heights.

Chapter 4.2: Recording Transactions and Maintaining Accurate Records

In the meticulous business world, every transaction plays a crucial role—a step that raises its significance on the ledger, molding the financial narrative of a company. For individuals specializing in financial record-keeping, such as Emily, meticulously documenting these transactions and upholding precise records is not merely a mundane task; it is a crucial responsibility that guarantees the trustworthiness and dependability of a company's financial information.

The Cornerstone of Double-Entry Accounting

Central to recording transactions is the fundamental principle of double-entry accounting. This bookkeeping method guarantees precision and uniformity by documenting each transaction in at least two accounts: a debit and a credit. This principle, which has been used for centuries, is credited to the Italian mathematician Luca Piccioli. It serves as the foundation for modern bookkeeping practices, offering a structure for arranging and summarizing financial information.

Emily found great satisfaction in mastering the principles of double-entry accounting. It was as if she was immersing herself in a new language filled with debits and credits, assets and liabilities, revenues and expenses. She meticulously recorded every transaction, ensuring that each followed the fundamental equation: Assets = Liabilities + Equity. Emily understood the importance of maintaining a delicate balance in the books. She knew accuracy and integrity were crucial for the financial records, whether it was recording revenue, expenses, or assets and liabilities.

Recording transactions required more than just adhering to the principles of double-entry accounting. It involved comprehending the essence of each transaction and categorizing it into suitable accounts. Emily learned about the various types of accounts, such as assets, liabilities, Equity, revenues, and expenses. She also learned how to classify transactions according to their nature and purpose. Emily understood the importance of recording every transaction accurately and promptly to ensure the company's financial position and performance were clearly and reliably represented.

Essential Tools for the Job: Accounting Software and Systems

In the digital age, bookkeepers have a valuable tool to assist them in recording transactions and ensuring the accuracy of their records: accounting software. These advanced programs streamline numerous tasks related to bookkeeping, including data entry, reconciliation, and reporting. This enables bookkeepers to dedicate their attention to more strategic aspects of their role.

Emily found accounting software incredibly valuable, revolutionizing her work process, enhancing her productivity, and minimizing the chances of mistakes and discrepancies in her records. Emily efficiently managed her clients' finances, utilizing automatic bank feeds, a customizable chart of accounts, and real-time reporting. This allowed her to provide timely and accurate information, enabling her clients to make well-informed decisions.

However, Emily understood that accounting software's effectiveness relied solely on the quality of the data it received. She understood the significance of maintaining precise records and ensuring that transactions were promptly and accurately recorded. Emily diligently maintained accurate and error-free records, giving her clients the confidence and peace of mind to manage their businesses effectively. From reconciling bank statements to verifying account balances and conducting audits, she left no stone unturned in her meticulous bookkeeping.

Effective Strategies for Maintaining Accurate Records

Emily excelled at understanding the intricacies of double-entry accounting and effectively utilized accounting software. She was meticulous in her record-keeping, always following best practices to maintain the utmost accuracy and integrity of her records. She ensured accuracy and integrity by implementing various measures, such as dividing responsibilities, obtaining authorizations for significant transactions, and establishing robust internal controls and protocols.

Emily meticulously maintained thorough records of every transaction, ensuring that she had a comprehensive audit trail and solid evidence to validate the accuracy of her documentation. Emily meticulously recorded and stored every transaction, ensuring they were easily accessible when needed.

Consistency played a crucial role in effective record-keeping. Emily understood the importance of maintaining precise records, so she established reliable practices and procedures for recording transactions, reconciling accounts, and generating reports. Emily was meticulous in her approach to record-keeping. She established a strict routine for entering and reconciling data, developed standardized templates and workflows, and regularly reviewed and audited her records. Her unwavering commitment to accuracy and reliability instilled confidence and trust in her clients, who relied on her expertise.

The Importance of Precise Documentation

As Emily pondered her role as a meticulous record keeper and the significance of documenting transactions and upholding precise records, she understood her work's significant influence on her clients' businesses. Emily's meticulous record-keeping skills played a crucial role in the success of her clients.

From helping small business owners stay on top of their expenses and cash flow to ensuring nonprofit organizations meet regulatory requirements and even guiding startup entrepreneurs through financial reporting, Emily's clients relied on her accurate and dependable records.

However, aside from the practical advantages of maintaining precise records, Emily also understood the importance of her role in establishing trust and credibility with her clients. Her meticulous attention to detail and prompt information delivery showcased her dedication to their prosperity and gained their faith and devotion in response. Emily's clients trusted her to handle all aspects of their financial needs, from preparing financial statements to offering advice on tax deductions and budgeting. Her expertise and professionalism were invaluable in helping them reach their financial goals.

As Emily looked ahead to the future, she anticipated that her position as a bookkeeper would continue to develop and become increasingly significant. With the business landscape becoming more intricate and cutthroat, the demand for precise and trustworthy financial data will only rise, highlighting the significance of her expertise and meticulousness. Emily was always dedicated to her clients, diligently keeping track of transactions and maintaining accurate records.

She understood the importance of providing her clients with the necessary information for success.

4.3 Introduction to Accounting Software: Enhancing Efficiency with Useful Tips and Tricks

In the dynamic world of bookkeeping and accounting, technology has become an essential companion, equipping bookkeepers such as Sarah with advanced tools to simplify their work, boost productivity, and ensure precision. Amid this technological revolution, accounting software has emerged as a powerful tool. It consists of a suite of programs that streamline and automate various tasks involved in bookkeeping, including data entry, reconciliation, and reporting. For Sarah, becoming proficient in accounting software was more than just acquiring a new skill; it was a gateway to endless opportunities and a complete revolution in her work approach.

Selecting the Perfect Accounting Software

Choosing the right tool for the job is crucial when harnessing the power of accounting software. With a wide array of options, including basic invoicing and expense tracking apps and comprehensive cloud-based accounting platforms, selecting the perfect software can feel overwhelming.

Through meticulous research and thoughtful deliberation, Sarah pinpointed the most significant features and functionalities for her and her clients. This enabled her to streamline her choices to a select few top contenders.

Sarah prioritized user-friendly design and easy access. She required a software solution that was easy to use and had a streamlined interface for efficient navigation and information retrieval. She required a software solution that offered remote accessibility, enabling her to work from any location and collaborate with clients in real time. After carefully considering various options, Sarah decided to go with a cloud-based accounting platform that aligned with her requirements and provided the necessary flexibility and scalability to support the growth of her business.

Getting Your Accounting Software Ready

After Sarah had selected accounting software, the subsequent task of setting up and configuring it was to tailor it according to her unique requirements and preferences. I had to create a chart of accounts, listing all the accounts and categories for classifying transactions. Additionally, I had to customize settings and preferences like currency, tax rates, and financial reporting formats. Sarah diligently imported the existing data and transactions from her clients' previous accounting systems, guaranteeing a seamless transition to the new software.

However, establishing accounting software required continuous effort and constant fine-tuning. Sarah diligently maintained and revised her chart of accounts to ensure it accurately captured her clients' changing business requirements and financial transactions. She meticulously tailored reports and dashboards to give her clients the necessary insights and information to make well-informed decisions and track their economic performance.

Streamlining Repetitive Tasks

One of the critical benefits of accounting software's strengths lies in its capacity to automate repetitive tasks and streamline repetitive processes, saving significant time and minimizing the chances of errors. For Sarah, this involved utilizing features like bank feeds, recurring transactions, and batch processing to streamline data entry, reconciliation, and reporting tasks. With the help of automation, Sarah could dedicate her time and efforts to more strategic aspects of her role, such as financial analysis, planning, and advisory services.

However, automation was more than a mere convenience; it completely revolutionized how Sarah and her clients operated. With the help of automation, Sarah successfully eliminated meticulously inputting data to maintain precision and consistency in her records. With the help of automation, Sarah efficiently detected and resolved discrepancies between bank statements and accounting records, guaranteeing the accuracy and reliability of her client's financial data. With the help of automation, Sarah effortlessly generated personalized reports and dashboards whenever needed, offering her clients immediate access to valuable information about their economic performance.

Streamlining the integration process with various tools and systems aside from automating routine tasks, accounting software also provides seamless integration with various tools and systems, enabling professionals like Sarah to optimize their workflow and boost efficiency. Think about how much easier it would be to run your finances with accounting software. It seamlessly integrates with payment processors, e-commerce platforms, and project management tools, allowing you to consolidate data and simplify your processes—no more tedious data entry by hand, and hello to improved accuracy and efficiency.

Achieving seamless integration was crucial for Sarah in streamlining her workflow and ensuring her clients had a smooth and cohesive experience. With the seamless integration of her accounting software and her clients' other business systems and tools, Sarah effortlessly streamlined data entry and maintained perfect synchronization across all systems. Sarah utilized various integrations to optimize her workflow and enhance the quality of service she provided to her clients. These integrations allowed her to effortlessly import sales data, synchronize expenses, and seamlessly integrate with payroll providers. As a result, Sarah's work became more efficient and reliable.

Keeping current with training and support

Like any other software tool, keeping up with training and support is crucial to making the most of accounting software. For Sarah, this involved utilizing training resources and tutorials provided by the software provider, interacting with others in internet communities and forums and exchanging helpful insights and strategies. Sarah diligently stayed up-to-date with software updates and new features, consistently reviewing release notes and participating in webinars and training sessions to keep informed about the latest enhancements and improvements.

However, Sarah thought the software provider's support was priceless. Whenever Sarah needed assistance, she could always count on the support team to promptly and effectively help her with any technical issues, user errors, or questions about software functionality. Through diligent communication and fostering a close partnership with the support team, Sarah triumphed over obstacles. She maximized the potential of her accounting software, guaranteeing a seamless and prosperous experience for herself and her clients.

In summary

As Sarah looked back on her experience of mastering accounting software and utilizing its capabilities to streamline her work and boost her efficiency, she couldn't help but feel a deep sense of accomplishment and contentment. She knew that by embracing the advancements in bookkeeping and adapting to the digital era, she had set herself up for triumph. With the appropriate software tools and practical strategies, Sarah was confident in expanding her business, delivering top-notch service to her clients, and accomplishing her objectives as a skilled bookkeeper. And as she gazed into the future, she was confident that

The possibilities seemed limitless as technology kept advancing and introducing new opportunities for professionals in bookkeeping.

Chapter 5:

Managing Clients

In managing finances, where strong relationships are crucial, becoming skilled in client management is vital for establishing trust, promoting teamwork, and achieving lasting success. For individuals with expertise in financial management, such as Emily, client management goes beyond simply handling numbers. It involves comprehending each client's requirements and objectives, offering customized service, and consistently delivering outstanding value.

Developing solid connections with clients is essential for achieving success.

Establishing and maintaining robust and enduring connections with clients is paramount in client management. Every client presents unique challenges, objectives, and expectations regardless of background or industry. Like a skilled bookkeeper, understanding clients' unique needs and goals allows customized services and solutions that provide the utmost value.

Emily believed in the importance of fostering strong client relationships, viewing it as a fundamental principle that shaped her approach to client management. She deeply understood the importance of trust, transparency, and open communication in building solid, long-lasting client relationships. With meticulous attention to detail, Emily carefully tended to her clients' concerns, diligently answering their questions and meeting their needs. This unwavering dedication allowed her to cultivate trust and credibility, ultimately earning her clients' unwavering confidence and loyalty.

Mastering the art of effective communication and collaboration is crucial in any professional setting.

Efficient communication is essential for effectively managing clients. Providing regular updates on financial records, simplifying accounting concepts, and offering strategic recommendations and insights are all crucial for keeping clients informed and engaged during the bookkeeping process.

Emily prioritized effective communication in her client management strategy. She meticulously maintained open lines of communication with her clients, utilizing various methods such as email, phone calls, and virtual meetings. She was always there to answer questions and address concerns, ensuring her clients felt supported and informed.

However, effective communication went beyond mere conversation—it also involved active listening. Emily was attentive to her client's needs and concerns, seeking feedback and input to ensure she met their expectations and provided the service they deserved. With a keen focus on her clients, Emily developed stronger connections, gained valuable insights into their businesses, and pinpointed opportunities for enhancement and expansion.

Offering Additional Services to Enhance Your Experience like a bookkeeper, professionals in this field offer a range of services beyond data entry, reconciliation, and reporting.

They can assist clients in reaching their financial objectives and fostering business expansion. Providing strategic advice on budgeting and forecasting, optimizing tax strategies, and assisting with financial planning and analysis can set bookkeepers apart from their competitors and strengthen client relationships.

Emily prioritized delivering services that added value to her clients as an integral part of her client management strategy. She meticulously analyzed her clients' objectives and dreams, pinpointing opportunities to offer extra guidance and specialized knowledge to ensure their success. Emily used her knowledge and expertise to guide and support her clients, whether helping a small business owner improve cash flow management, assisting a nonprofit organization with fundraising strategy, or guiding a startup entrepreneur in securing financing. She was dedicated to helping her clients achieve their goals.

Mastering the art of managing expectations and gracefully navigating through challenges is crucial.

Just like a meticulous record-keeper, it is crucial to effectively handle client relationships by setting clear expectations and tackling obstacles proactively and openly. Being organized and proactive is essential for effective client management. This includes setting clear deadlines and deliverables, communicating potential delays or obstacles, and promptly addressing issues and concerns.

Emily excelled at managing expectations and handling challenges as part of her client management strategy. She ensured that her clients were well-informed from the start, providing them with a comprehensive breakdown of the services, schedule, and costs straightforwardly and openly. She maintained regular communication with her clients, ensuring that clients were regularly updated on the status of their projects, addressing any concerns or issues, and seeking feedback on her performance.

However, when faced with challenges, as is common in any business relationship, Emily promptly tackled them without hesitation. Emily diligently addressed issues, ensuring the client's needs were met and resolved promptly. With a keen eye for detail and a commitment to precision, Emily solidified her client connections and instilled steadfast faith in her bookkeeping prowess.

Final Thoughts: The Importance of Client Management

As Emily contemplated becoming a skilled client manager, she recognized the significant influence that cultivating strong connections and mastering communication had on her achievements in the field. With a strong focus on precision and unwavering commitment to her clients, Emily established herself as a trusted partner in managing their financial records. Through open communication and a commitment to excellence, she successfully grew her bookkeeping business, positively impacting the lives of her clients.

Emily's approach to client management went beyond mere business strategy. It was a way of thinking, a set of principles, and a dedication to providing exceptional service that influenced every aspect of her work. Emily understood the importance of building solid and lasting relationships with her clients. She was dedicated to providing personalized service, offering strategic advice, and always going above and beyond to exceed their expectations.

Emily anticipated the future with a sense of excitement, fully aware that her journey had only just commenced. With a strong focus on client management, she was determined to drive her business forward, attract more clients, and reach her professional goals as a bookkeeper. With every new client she took under her wing, she understood the potential to make a meaningful difference and assist them in reaching their financial aspirations.

5.1 Onboarding Clients: Establishing Expectations and Agreements

In bookkeeping, where numbers come alive and transactions weave tales, bringing on new clients is like setting the stage for a prosperous journey. For individuals in the role of a bookkeeper, such as Emily, the journey commences by setting up explicit expectations and agreements rather than immediately diving into number crunching. It's all about embarking on a voyage of teamwork, effective communication, and shared objectives, guaranteeing that the financial manager and the client are on the same page right from the start.

The Importance of Onboarding

The onboarding process is crucial for establishing a solid foundation for the client relationship. It's the moment when two parties meet to develop the rules of engagement, clarify expectations, and set the stage for a productive partnership. By dedicating time and energy to the onboarding process, individuals in the role of a bookkeeper can establish a solid starting point, setting the stage for a fruitful and mutually advantageous partnership.

Emily approached the onboarding process with meticulous attention to detail, ensuring that every task was completed flawlessly. She understood the importance of building trust, fostering open communication, and showcasing her unwavering dedication to her clients' success. With a good grasp of what her clients want, goals, and concerns, Emily customizes her services to meet their specific requirements. This ensures they receive the personalized attention and support they deserve immediately.

Establishing Clear Expectations

Setting clear expectations is crucial in the onboarding process. This requires a thorough understanding of the services and deliverables and clear definitions of roles, responsibilities, and timelines. Through effective communication and setting clear expectations from the start, individuals in the role of a bookkeeper can reduce the chances of misunderstandings and make sure that all parties agree regarding their goals and objectives.

Emily made it a top priority to establish clear expectations during her onboarding process. She ensured that her clients understood the extent of her services by clearly and concisely explaining what they could anticipate from her and what she anticipated from them in exchange. Emily was meticulous in her approach, leaving no room for confusion. She set clear deadlines for submitting financial documents, established a regular communication schedule, and provided a transparent process for reviewing and approving financial reports. Her clients always knew exactly what to expect from the start.

Establishing Efficient Communication Channels

Efficient communication channels are crucial for a successful client relationship, and the onboarding process presents the ideal chance to establish clear lines of communication. Establishing effective communication channels is vital for bookkeepers to stay connected with their clients.

Effective communication channels are essential from the beginning, whether through email, phone calls, video conferences, or project management tools.

Emily prioritized establishing effective communication channels during her onboarding process. She was meticulous in ensuring that she had thorough discussions with her clients regarding their communication preferences and availability for meetings and calls. She established regular check-ins and status updates to inform her clients about the progress of their bookkeeping tasks and to address any questions or concerns they might have had.

Crafting Agreements and Contracts

Just like a meticulous record-keeper, the onboarding process includes the creation of formal agreements that spell out the terms and conditions of the client relationship, setting expectations and establishing communication channels. This encompasses various aspects, such as the range of services provided, the terms and conditions for fees and payments, agreements regarding confidentiality, and mechanisms for resolving disputes.

Emily considered creating agreements and contracts to be an essential part of her onboarding process. She diligently collaborated with her clients to develop tailored agreements that captured their distinct requirements and desires, guaranteeing the safeguarding of both parties and establishing well-defined protocols for addressing any potential conflicts or challenges that may arise throughout their partnership.

Teaching Clients

Finally, the onboarding process allows bookkeepers to inform their clients about the significance of their services and the need for precise financial records. Bookkeepers must educate clients about their role and the importance of accurate financial records. This helps clients understand the value they provide.

Emily prioritized educating her clients as a crucial aspect of her onboarding process. She thoroughly explained to her clients the significance of maintaining precise financial records and how they could reap the rewards of her expertise.

She shared valuable advice and strategies for managing financial records and staying organized in bookkeeping responsibilities. This empowered them to have a firm grip on their finances and make well-informed business decisions.

In Closing: Recognizing the Significance of Onboarding

As Emily pondered her onboarding process, she understood the importance of building a solid base for a fruitful client relationship right from the start. With a meticulous approach, Emily established solid and enduring relationships with her clients, paving the way for a productive and mutually advantageous partnership. She achieved this by setting clear expectations, implementing effective communication channels, formalizing agreements, and educating her clients about the value of her services. With a keen eye on the future, she was confident that her unwavering dedication to providing top-notch onboarding services would pave the way for prosperous client relationships and the steady expansion of her business.

5.2 Communication Strategies for Developing Solid Client Relationships

In the world of meticulous record-keeping, where the art of balancing numbers and storytelling intertwines, the key to triumph lies in skillful communication. For someone experienced in bookkeeping, such as Sarah, developing practical communication skills goes beyond simply relaying information. It involves establishing trust, promoting teamwork, and cultivating enduring client connections.

In this sub-chapter, we'll delve into the essential communication strategies that can help foster strong and long-lasting relationships between bookkeepers and their clients.

Appreciating the Significance of Communication

People must learn to talk to each other clearly to build good relationships. And successful client relationships. It is crucial in connecting the bookkeeper and client, fostering clear communication, transparency, and a shared understanding throughout the process. Through effective communication, bookkeepers can establish trust, inspire confidence, and showcase their dedication to their clients' prosperity.

Sarah valued effective communication as a fundamental principle that shaped her client interactions. She understood the importance of effective communication in building connections, resolving issues, and promoting teamwork. She always prioritized open and transparent communication with her clients.

Creating Effective Lines of Communication

Establishing precise and efficient communication channels is crucial for effective communication. Just like a bookkeeper, it's essential to maintain open lines of communication with clients and be readily available and responsive to their needs, whether through email, phone calls, video conferences, or project management tools.

Sarah made it a top priority to establish clear communication channels in her client relationships. She ensured that she had open lines of communication with her clients, taking into account their preferred methods and availability for meetings and calls. In addition, she established regular check-ins and status updates to ensure her clients were well informed about the progress of their bookkeeping tasks and to address any questions or concerns they may have had.

Practicing active listening and showing empathy

Efficient communication requires a mutual exchange of information, with bookkeepers skilled in verbal expression and attentive listening. Being attentive and genuinely understanding the client's needs, concerns, and motivations is crucial to effective communication. Through active and empathetic listening, bookkeepers can showcase their dedication to their client's success and establish a strong connection and trust.

Sarah prioritized active listening as a critical component of her communication approach. She was meticulous in her approach, attentively listening to her clients' concerns and feedback. She asked insightful questions to understand their needs and preferences better. She had a knack for understanding her clients' perspectives and points of view, always putting herself in their shoes and showing empathy. With a keen ear and genuine understanding, Sarah fostered deeper connections with her clients, ensuring they received the individualized care and assistance they deserved.

Establishing and setting clear expectations is crucial.

To communicate well, it's essential to be clear about what you expect. Communicating the scope of services and deliverables and defining roles, responsibilities, and timelines is critical. Through effective communication and setting clear expectations from the start, individuals in the role of a bookkeeper can reduce the chances of clarity and interpretation. People can all understand what's going on about their goals and objectives.

Maintaining clear expectations was of utmost importance for Sarah in her client relationships. She ensured that her clients understood the extent of her services by clearly and concisely explaining what they could anticipate from her and what she anticipated from them in exchange. With meticulous attention to detail, Sarah established clear expectations for her clients. She set deadlines for financial document submissions, established regular communication, and outlined a transparent process for reviewing and approving financial reports. Her clients always knew exactly what to expect from the start.

Ensuring Consistent Communication and Input

Maintaining open lines of communication is crucial in ensuring that clients are kept in the loop regarding the status of their bookkeeping tasks. Providing regular updates and feedback helps address any queries or concerns they may have. With meticulous attention to detail and thorough record-keeping, bookkeepers can showcase their dedication to their clients' prosperity and foster a sense of trust and assurance in their skills.

For Sarah, maintaining a meticulous record of updates and feedback was essential to her communication strategy. She diligently kept her clients in the loop, ensuring they were always up to date on the progress of their bookkeeping tasks. Regular status updates and reports were provided to inform them of the latest developments. She actively sought feedback from her clients, valuing their input and suggestions for improvement. With meticulous attention to detail,

Sarah maintained open lines of communication with her clients, fostering stronger connections and ensuring their satisfaction.

Dealing with conflicts and addressing concerns

Conflicts and concerns are bound to arise in any client relationship, and it's crucial to have open and effective communication to deal with these issues promptly and productively. By openly addressing conflicts and concerns, individuals in the role of a bookkeeper can show their dedication to their client's satisfaction and strive to address problems in a manner that is advantageous for all parties involved.

Resolving conflicts and addressing concerns were critical components of Sarah's communication strategy. She was diligent in handling any issues or concerns in her client relationships, always striving to address them promptly and professionally. She took the time to investigate the underlying causes of the problems and worked closely with her clients to resolve them.

With sharp attention to detail and a talent for resolving financial disputes, Sarah approached conflicts with an open mind and a willingness to listen, ensuring that her clients felt heard and valued.

Final Thoughts: The Impact of Effective Communication

As Sarah pondered her communication strategies for fostering solid client relationships, she recognized the significant influence that effective communication had on her achievements as a bookkeeper. With meticulous attention to detail and dedication to her clients, Sarah established a solid foundation of trust and confidence. She fostered strong and enduring relationships with her clients through effective communication, active listening, and prompt resolution of conflicts. With a keen eye for detail and a dedication to effective communication, she confidently anticipated a prosperous future. Her unwavering commitment to excellence would undoubtedly lead to the triumph of her client projects and the expansion of her business.

5.3 Dealing with Challenging Clients and Resolving Conflicts in a Professional Manner

Within the complex web of client relationships, there comes a point where bookkeepers may encounter challenging clients or confront conflicts that jeopardize the partnership. Dealing with challenging clients and resolving disputes professionally is an essential skill for bookkeepers to acquire. Whether it's a result of miscommunication, conflicting expectations, or unexpected obstacles, mastering this ability is vital.

This section will delve into successful approaches for handling difficult circumstances with poise, expertise, and honesty.

Navigating Challenging Clients

Dealing with challenging clients can be difficult, ranging from being excessively demanding or controlling to needing to be more responsive and resistant to change. Understanding the underlying reasons behind challenging behavior is crucial for successfully handling these clients and finding favorable resolutions to conflicts. Handling these situations with empathy and understanding is vital, acknowledging that challenging behavior often arises from deep-seated fears, concerns, or frustrations.

Dealing with challenging clients was an unavoidable aspect of Sarah's role as a bookkeeper. She dealt with clients who needed more organization, doubted her expertise, and clients who were hesitant to embrace new processes or technologies. Seeing these clients as valuable learning experiences, Sarah embraced each interaction as an opportunity to improve her communication skills, develop resilience, and gain a deeper understanding of client needs and motivations.

Establishing clear boundaries and effectively managing expectations

Establishing clear boundaries and effectively managing client expectations is critical to successfully handling demanding clients. This requires effective communication of the services provided, clear expectations for communication and collaboration, and establishing protocols for resolving any concerns or conflicts. Through effective boundary-setting and proactive expectation management, individuals with expertise in financial record-keeping can reduce the likelihood of miscommunication and foster a shared understanding of objectives and goals.

As a meticulous organizer, Sarah prioritized setting boundaries and managing expectations in her client management strategy. She ensured that her clients understood the extent of her services by clearly and concisely explaining what she could and could not do for them. She implemented protocols for communication, establishing clear expectations for response times and availability for meetings and calls. With a meticulous approach, Sarah avoided potential conflicts by establishing clear boundaries and managing expectations. She promptly and professionally handled any issues that did arise.

Practicing active listening and empathy

Handling the situation with empathy and a deep understanding is crucial when dealing with challenging clients or conflicts. Attention to the client's words is essential, but it's equally vital to grasp their deeper needs, worries, and motivations. Through active and empathetic listening, bookkeepers can showcase their dedication to their client's success and establish a strong connection and trust, even under challenging circumstances.

For Sarah, maintaining a solid focus on attentive listening and displaying genuine empathy were critical elements of her strategy for effectively managing challenging clients. With a keen eye for detail and a commitment to professionalism, Sarah approached criticism and resistance with an open mind. She actively listened to her clients' concerns and feedback, striving to understand their perspectives better. She keenly understood her clients' perspectives and was always empathetic towards their frustrations and challenges. With a keen ear and a compassionate approach, Sarah developed more profound connections with her clients and discovered effective resolutions to their concerns.

Ensuring a high level of professionalism and integrity

When faced with challenging clients or conflicts, it is crucial always to uphold professionalism and integrity. Maintaining a sense of calm and composure, even when faced with difficult situations, and approaching challenges with patience, diplomacy, and grace is essential. It also involves maintaining high ethical standards and values, even in the face of pressure or temptation to compromise.

For Sarah, upholding a high professionalism and integrity standard was essential. She handled every interaction with her clients meticulously and diligently, regardless of the situation. With a knack for composure, Sarah adeptly navigated challenging situations, always seeking fair and equitable resolutions for all parties involved, even when dealing with demanding clients or conflicts. With her sharp focus on every detail and unwavering dedication to ethical practices, Sarah established herself as a reliable consultant, garnering the admiration and loyalty of her clientele.

Striving for a positive outcome through effective communication

When dealing with challenging clients, it's crucial to tackle conflicts directly by fostering open and transparent communication. This requires effectively communicating concerns or grievances, striving to comprehend the other party's viewpoint, and cooperating to discover a mutually agreeable solution. With a mindset of openness and cooperation, individuals can transform challenging situations into valuable opportunities for growth and learning.

For Sarah, maintaining open lines of communication proved essential in resolving conflicts with challenging clients. Like a meticulous record-keeper, Sarah took a proactive and transparent approach to dealing with issues. She genuinely tried understanding her clients' concerns and finding mutually agreeable solutions. She fostered an atmosphere of trust and understanding where her clients felt comfortable sharing their thoughts and emotions. This allowed for open and productive conversations where valuable feedback could be exchanged. Through effective communication, Sarah successfully resolved conflicts with challenging clients and built stronger relationships with them.

Recognizing the right time to step back

At times, even after considerable effort to resolve conflicts and address concerns, it may become evident that the client relationship is no longer viable. Knowing when to walk away and gracefully end the partnership is crucial. There are a few options to consider in this situation. One possibility is to end the contract in a friendly manner. Another option is to suggest a different service provider who better fits the client. Lastly, you could agree to go separate ways and find new opportunities.

Recognizing time to step back was challenging yet crucial for Sarah. Despite her diligent attempts to resolve conflicts and address concerns, there were moments when it became evident that the client relationship was no longer sustainable.

Instead of dragging it out, Sarah made the tough call to terminate the contract and gracefully end the partnership. With meticulous attention to detail, she effortlessly maintained her professionalism and integrity, allowing her to dedicate her energy to serving clients who were a better match for her exceptional services.

Final Thoughts: Dealing with Challenging Clients and Resolving Conflicts

As Sarah reflected on her encounters with demanding clients and disagreements, she understood the significance of maintaining patience, empathy, and resilience when dealing with these complex circumstances. With sharp attention to detail and a talent for organization, Sarah successfully navigated challenging client situations and effectively resolved conflicts. She skillfully set boundaries, managed expectations, and maintained a professional and trustworthy demeanor. She fostered open communication and built strong relationships by actively listening and showing empathy. Sarah knew when to disengage to guarantee the optimal result for everyone involved gracefully. As she gazed into the future, she realized that these experiences had bolstered her strength and resilience, enhancing her ability to navigate the intricacies of client relationships and forge enduring partnerships along the way.

Chapter 6:

Growing Your Business

As an entrepreneur, there comes a crucial moment when a small venture shows signs of growth and potential for expansion. Expanding their operations is a significant achievement for individuals who run their businesses and reflects their tireless efforts, commitment, and forward-thinking mindset. This chapter will explore the strategies and factors to consider when expanding a bookkeeping business. This includes broadening service offerings, hiring more staff, and utilizing technology to streamline operations.

The Vision of Growth

Scaling a business goes beyond mere financial gains and operational expansion. It involves bringing to life a vision of growth and seizing new opportunities. It's all about cultivating an idea and transforming it into a thriving business that positively affects the lives of both clients and employees. Emily was driven by a strong vision of growth, which motivated her to constantly push the boundaries and strive for excellence in all her endeavors.

Expanding our service offerings

Expanding service offerings is crucial for scaling a bookkeeping business. This allows you to meet clients' changing needs and attract new customers. As a business owner, consider expanding your offerings to include services like tax preparation, financial planning, or business consulting. Alternatively, you could explore new industries or market segments and develop specialized services to meet their unique needs.

Emily saw expanding her service offerings as a natural progression in her journey as a bookkeeper. As a savvy entrepreneur, she continuously sought innovative ways to enhance her clients' experience. This led her to expand her services, including strategic financial planning and expert tax optimization, ensuring her clients received maximum value. With the expansion of her service offerings, Emily successfully attracted new clients, strengthened her relationships with existing clients, and positioned her business for long-term success.

Considering the need to expand the workforce

Running a bookkeeping business comes with its own set of challenges as it continues to expand. The owner's time and resources become more and more stretched. Many bookkeepers hire extra staff to handle the increasing workload and ensure that service quality remains consistently high. Consider hiring bookkeeping assistants, administrative staff, or additional bookkeepers to manage client accounts.

Emily recognized the importance of expanding her workforce to grow her business. As her client base grew and her workload intensified, she realized she couldn't handle everything alone. With the help of a talented and committed team, Emily successfully delegated tasks, optimized operations, and dedicated her efforts to expanding the business and providing excellent service to clients.

Harnessing the power of technology

In today's modern era, technology is essential for the growth of any business, including bookkeeping. Utilizing technology to streamline operations, automate repetitive tasks, and enhance efficiency allows bookkeepers to allocate their time and resources towards more strategic activities and value-added services.

Emily found that incorporating technology into her business was pivotal in her quest for growth. As a savvy entrepreneur, she decided to invest in cloud-based accounting software. This allowed her to effortlessly access client data from any location and collaborate with clients in real time. She efficiently automated routine tasks like data entry and reconciliation, allowing her to dedicate more time to strategic activities such as financial analysis and planning. With the help of technology, Emily successfully expanded her business, achieving greater efficiency and effectiveness.

Building Strategic Partnerships

Building strategic partnerships with other professionals and service providers in related fields is essential for scaling a bookkeeping business. Forming alliances with accounting firms, financial advisors, or software vendors can be beneficial for expanding services and reaching new markets and client segments.

Emily understood the importance of establishing strategic partnerships to fuel her growth strategy. She partnered with accounting firms and financial advisors to provide customers with various financial planning services. By leveraging their expertise and resources, she was able to deliver additional value. She also collaborated with software vendors to provide integrated solutions that optimized her clients' operations and enhanced efficiency. Through establishing strategic partnerships, Emily broadened her range of services, reached out to a broader client base, and positioned her business for ongoing expansion and prosperity.

It's essential to spend money on marketing and branding for any entrepreneur or business owner. It is necessary to allocate resources to these areas to effectively promote products or services and build a strong brand identity. By strategically investing in marketing and branding, businesses can increase their visibility, attract new customers, and drive growth and success.

When running a bookkeeping business, it is crucial to prioritize marketing and branding initiatives. These efforts will help increase visibility, attract fresh clientele, and set your business apart from competitors. Developing a solid brand identity, creating a professional website and marketing materials, and implementing targeted marketing campaigns are essential to reaching potential clients.

Emily understood the importance of investing in marketing and branding to drive her growth strategy. She collaborated with a designer to develop a polished logo and branding materials that captured her unique vision and identity. She invested in a website and established a solid social media presence to effectively showcase her services and expertise, ultimately attracting new clients. Through strategic investments in marketing and branding, Emily successfully increased awareness of her business, attracted a fresh clientele, and solidified her reputation as a reliable expert in her industry.

Measuring and monitoring performance is crucial for any business owner. It helps you keep track of success, find places to improve, and make intelligent choices. Regularly analyzing key metrics and data can find helpful information about your strategies and tactics. This enables you to make necessary adjustments and optimize your business operations for success.

As a business owner, measuring and monitoring a bookkeeping business's performance as it scales to ensure sustainable and profitable growth is crucial. As a business owner, keeping an eye on key performance indicators like revenue, profit margins, client retention rates, and employee productivity is essential. These metrics can help you identify areas of strength and areas that could use some improvement.

Emily understood the importance of measuring and monitoring performance as a crucial element of her growth strategy. She established systems and processes to monitor important metrics like revenue growth, client satisfaction, and employee productivity. This enabled her to evaluate the overall performance of her business and make well-informed choices regarding resource allocation and strategic focus. With a keen eye on performance, Emily pinpointed her business's strengths and weaknesses. By optimizing her operations, she strategically positioned her business for long-term success.

Final Thoughts: The Path to Expansion

Emily contemplated her journey of expanding her bookkeeping business and acknowledged that the road to growth was often filled with obstacles and uncertainties. It took a lot of commitment, perseverance, and readiness to adapt to new situations and unknowns. Through unwavering dedication and a strong sense of purpose, Emily conquered obstacles, capitalized on favorable circumstances, and established a prosperous enterprise that positively influenced the well-being of both her customers and staff.

As she gazed into the future, she realized the path to success was never-ending. There were always uncharted territories to discover, obstacles to overcome, and prospects to chase after. With her strong vision, unwavering passion, and relentless commitment to excellence, Emily was sure that she could steadily expand her business and accomplish her objectives, gradually but surely.

6.1 Enhancing Operational Efficiency for Business Expansion

In the fast-paced realm of entrepreneurship, where every second counts and effectiveness are paramount, optimizing processes is more than just a trendy phrase—it is an essential requirement for thriving and achieving goals. For bookkeepers such as Emily, who are navigating the complex world of scaling their business, the importance of streamlining operations goes beyond mere convenience. It is about establishing a solid foundation for future growth and expansion. As a business owner, it is essential to explore the strategies and techniques to help bookkeepers streamline their operations and set the stage for future success.

The Importance of Efficiency

Efficiency is crucial for bookkeepers who want to grow their business. As a savvy entrepreneur, you understand the value of optimizing your operations and maximizing productivity. In a fast-paced world where time is limited, and resources are valuable, every moment spent on manual processes, repetitive tasks, or ineffective workflows is a lost chance to propel your business forward. Understanding the importance of efficiency, Emily embarked on a mission to optimize her operations, fully aware that this would enhance productivity and profitability and pave the way for her business to thrive in the long run.

Embracing the Potential of Technology

Utilizing technology is a highly effective method for streamlining operations. Technology has the potential to revolutionize the way bookkeepers work, enabling them to automate repetitive tasks, streamline processes, and improve efficiency. From cloud-based accounting software to automation tools and project management platforms, there are various options available.

Emily found that incorporating technology into her operations was pivotal in her efforts to make things more efficient. As a savvy entrepreneur, she decided to invest in cloud-based accounting software. This software allowed her to access client data from any location, at any hour, and work with clients in real-time.

She streamlined her operations by automating routine tasks like data entry, reconciliation, and report generation. This allowed her to dedicate more time to strategic activities and value-added services.

Streamlining Work Processes

Another critical strategy for streamlining operations is optimizing workflows and leveraging technology. This requires thoroughly examining current processes, pinpointing areas of inefficiency and congestion, and implementing enhancements to optimize workflow and boost productivity.

Emily was constantly refining and improving workflows. She regularly reviewed her team's processes, seeking feedback from team members and clients to pinpoint areas for improvement. She made changes to streamline workflows, eliminate redundant tasks, and automate repetitive processes, ensuring that her team worked efficiently and effectively.

Empowering Team Members

Efficiently managing operations involves more than just implementing technology and processes—it also entails enabling team members to unleash their maximum potential. Through the provision of training, resources, and support, bookkeepers can empower their team members. This empowerment allows individuals to take ownership of their work, make well-informed decisions, and ultimately contribute to the business's overall success.

Emily prioritized empowering her team members as she worked to streamline operations. She ensured her team received training and development opportunities to improve their skills and knowledge, enabling them to handle challenging tasks and take on additional responsibilities with self-assurance. She encouraged people to work together and come up with new ideas. She encouraged team members to freely share ideas and insights to improve processes and drive efficiency.

Adopting a culture of always getting better is essential for success.

As a business owner, it's essential to understand that streamlining operations is a never-ending process that demands a dedication to constantly improving. With an eye on improving and growing, bookkeepers can keep their operations flexible and ready to adapt to market changes, client demands, and technological advancements.

Emily prioritized a culture of continuous improvement to streamline operations effectively. She motivated her team members to embrace change and experimentation, question the norm, and actively pursue opportunities for innovation and progress. She actively sought feedback from clients and stakeholders, valuing their insights to make improvements and streamline processes.

Conclusion: Setting the Stage for Expansion

Emily's reflection on her journey to streamline operations for growth revealed that the path to success could have been smoother. Still, it proved worthwhile despite the various challenges and obstacles encountered. Through the strategic use of technology, efficient workflow management, empowering team members, and fostering a culture of constant improvement, Emily successfully streamlined her operations, enhancing efficiency and positioning her business for long-term growth and prosperity. As she gazed into the future, she understood that the path to improving efficiency was far from complete. There were still uncharted technologies to investigate, processes to fine-tune, and exciting prospects to chase after. With her strong vision, unwavering determination, and relentless pursuit of excellence, Emily was sure she could further optimize her operations and set the stage for a promising and prosperous future.

6.2 Hiring Assistance: Virtual Assistants, Contractors, and Employees

In the fast-paced realm of business growth, the demand for support frequently becomes an unavoidable truth. As bookkeepers such as Sarah experiences a surge in workload and witness their businesses thriving, hiring more assistance becomes vital for maintaining growth and securing ongoing prosperity. As a business owner, it's essential to consider the different options for hiring assistance in bookkeeping. This sub-chapter will explore the benefits and considerations of working with virtual assistants, contractors, and employees.

The Evolution of the Bookkeeping Business

As a business owner, Sarah's journey of building her bookkeeping business has been an exhilarating rollercoaster ride, filled with moments of success and obstacles to overcome. What began as a one-person operation has flourished into a successful business with a growing customer base and an expanding range of services. However, with the increasing demands of her business, Sarah faced the challenge of juggling multiple responsibilities and ensuring that she could meet the high service standards her clients were accustomed to.

Understanding the importance of getting help was the initial milestone in Sarah's quest to expand her business. She recognized the importance of not shouldering the entire workload herself and realized that hiring extra assistance was crucial for maintaining growth and securing the future success of her business. With many options, Sarah was challenged to choose the most suitable path for her business.

The Emergence of Virtual Assistants

Virtual assistants have become increasingly popular among bookkeepers who want to streamline operations and delegate administrative tasks. These remote workers offer various services, such as email management, appointment scheduling, invoicing, and data entry. This enables bookkeepers to dedicate their time and effort to more strategic activities and tasks involving client interaction.

As a business owner, Sarah found that hiring a virtual assistant was a game-changer in her efforts to streamline operations and scale her business. She hired a virtual assistant to handle administrative tasks like her inbox, scheduling appointments, and organizing client files. As a business owner, Sarah could leverage her virtual assistant's assistance to reclaim precious time for strategic growth, client care, and service expansion.

Contractors offer a high level of flexibility.

Contractors provide bookkeepers with a flexible option for hiring assistance as needed, similar to how business owners would approach it. Contractors offer their specialized skills and expertise for specific projects or tasks, providing bookkeepers with access to additional resources without the need to hire full-time employees on a long-term basis.

Working with contractors was a strategic decision for Sarah, enabling her to tap into specialized expertise and enhance the efficiency of her business. She enlisted the help of contractors to support various projects, including tax preparation, financial analysis, and software implementation. By utilizing their expertise, she was able to provide enhanced value to her clients. Through collaboration with contractors, Sarah successfully broadened her range of services, catering to the varied requirements of her clients, and set her business on a path of ongoing expansion and prosperity.

The Importance of Employee Stability

As a business owner, it's essential to consider the benefits of hiring full-time employees for bookkeeping. While virtual assistants and contractors offer flexibility and scalability, having a dedicated team of employees provides the stability and consistency needed to support long-term growth and sustainability. Employees are committed to the business, ensuring consistent and dependable day-to-day operations.

This fosters a strong team dynamic with a shared vision and common values.

As a business owner, Sarah considered hiring full-time employees a significant milestone in her journey towards scaling her business. She hired more staff to help with client management, bookkeeping tasks, and business development, forming a dedicated team that shared her vision and commitment to excellence. Thanks to her employees' dedication and hard work, Sarah successfully grew her client base, expanded her range of services, and established her business as a prominent player in the industry.

Considerations for Hiring Assistance

When considering hiring assistance, bookkeepers should keep several important factors in mind. Various factors, including budget, workload, skill requirements, and long-term goals, will all contribute to determining the most suitable approach for each business. It's crucial to thoroughly analyze the business's unique requirements, assess the resources, and meticulously consider what's good and bad about each option before concluding.

For Sarah, choosing to hire assistance was a serious matter. She meticulously assessed her options, considering her financial resources, the demands of her workload, and the necessary skills to sustain her business. She carefully considered the advantages and disadvantages of working with virtual assistants, contractors, and employees, ultimately combining all three to suit her requirements best.

In conclusion: Finding the Right Fit

Reflecting on her journey to scale her bookkeeping business, Sarah realized that hiring assistance was a crucial turning point in her entrepreneurial endeavor. With the support of virtual assistants, contractors, and employees, Sarah successfully optimized her operations, broadened her range of services, and positioned her business for sustainable growth and prosperity. As she gazed into the future, she understood how important it is to find the right match for her business. It wasn't just about reaching her goals and bringing her vision of creating a prosperous and enduring enterprise to life.

6.3 Expanding Your Service Offerings and Reaching New Customers

In the ever-changing world of bookkeeping, adapting and evolving is crucial for staying ahead of the competition. For bookkeepers such as Emily, who are navigating the complexities of scaling their business, diversifying service offerings and expanding reach, represent opportunities for growth and essential strategies for staying relevant in a competitive market.

In this section, we will delve into the significance of diversification and expansion, the advantages they can offer to a bookkeeping business, and practical approaches for putting them into action.

The Strength of Diversification

For a bookkeeping business to thrive and stay ahead of the competition, expanding and diversifying the range of services is crucial. By expanding their service offerings, bookkeepers can attract a broader client base, strengthen connections with current clients, and stand out from competitors. Embracing diversification enables bookkeepers to explore fresh sources of income and stay flexible in response to shifting market dynamics and client demands.

Emily saw the value in expanding her range of services as she worked to grow her business. She understood the changing needs of her clients and aimed to adapt her business to meet them proactively. Through the expansion of her service offerings to include tax preparation, financial planning, and business consulting, Emily was able to offer more comprehensive solutions to her clients' financial needs. This helped her establish herself as a trusted advisor and partner.

Expanding Your Reach

Expanding reach is a crucial strategy for scaling a bookkeeping business, as it allows for more significant growth and success. With the ability to tap into untapped markets and reach new client segments, bookkeepers have the potential to expand their business and make a more significant impact in the industry.

Expanding your reach can involve:

- Targeting new industries or geographic regions.
- Utilizing technology to connect with remote clients.
- Establishing strategic partnerships with other businesses or service providers.

Emily was determined to broaden her reach as she worked towards growing her business. She understood the potential for expansion beyond her current market and was eager to explore new opportunities for business growth. Emily successfully grew her customer base by using technology to connect with clients in remote locations and establishing valuable collaborations with professionals in complementary industries. She expanded the reach of her business, setting the stage for sustained prosperity.

Benefits of Diversification and Expansion

Expanding service offerings and reaching a wider audience can provide numerous advantages for individuals running their businesses. Here are some examples:

Number 1. By expanding their service offerings and tapping into untapped markets, bookkeepers can open up new avenues for generating revenue and ultimately boost their total revenue potential.

Number 2. Because they provide a wider range of services, bookkeepers can strengthen their connections with current clients and better address their financial requirements. Additionally, it can attract new clients looking for a broader selection of services.

Number 3. By differentiating themselves from competitors and offering unique value propositions, bookkeepers can gain a competitive advantage in the market and position themselves as industry leaders.

Number 4. Being able to adapt is crucial for bookkeepers. Diversification and expansion help them stay relevant in a constantly changing market. By meeting the evolving needs of their clients and keeping up with industry dynamics, bookkeepers can ensure their long-term success and sustainability.

Number 5. Exploring new markets and service offerings opens up opportunities for innovation and creativity, allowing bookkeepers always to be ahead of the curve and in the lead of industry trends.

Practical Strategies for Implementation

Successfully implementing diversification and expansion strategies necessitates meticulous planning, flawless execution, and thorough evaluation. Here are some practical methods for bookkeepers who want to broaden their service offerings and extend their reach:

Number 1. Conduct comprehensive market research to identify potential opportunities for diversification and expansion. Examine market trends, competitor offerings, and client needs to identify possible gaps or unexplored opportunities.

Number 2. Client Feedback: Request input from current clients to gain insight into their requirements, preferences, and challenges. Utilize this feedback to make informed decisions regarding new service offerings and strategies for expansion.

Number 3. Forming strategic partnerships with other businesses or service providers in related fields can help you expand your reach and access new markets. Work together on joint marketing initiatives, referral programs, or bundled service offerings to maximize impact and effectiveness.

Number 4. Utilize technology to optimize operations and enhance communication with clients in remote locations. Investing in cloud-based accounting software, communication tools, and marketing automation platforms can significantly improve efficiency and scalability.

Number 5. Continuously assessing the performance of new service offerings and expansion initiatives is crucial to ensure they meet objectives and provide value to clients. Adapt strategies as necessary in response to feedback and changes in the market.

Conclusion: Embracing Growth and Opportunity

Emily contemplates her journey of expanding service offerings and reaching a wider audience. She acknowledges the significance of embracing growth and seizing opportunities in the constantly evolving bookkeeping industry. Emily successfully grew her business with a diverse range of services, expanding into new markets and staying ahead of the competition. She established herself as a prominent figure in the industry. As she gazes into the future, she understands that the path of diversification and growth must still be completed. There are still uncharted markets to venture into, untapped clients to cater to, and fresh opportunities to chase after. With her strong vision, unwavering determination, and relentless pursuit of excellence, Emily is poised to grow and thrive in the ever-changing realm of bookkeeping.

Chapter 7:

Maximizing Profitability

In the fast-paced realm of entrepreneurship, where every choice carries weight and every cent holds significance, the quest for profitability is an ongoing expedition. For individuals like Sarah, who have devoted themselves to establishing thriving businesses, maximizing profitability is not just a goal but a strategic imperative that influences every aspect of their operations. In this chapter, we'll delve into the essential strategies and tactics that bookkeepers can utilize to enhance profitability. This includes fine-tuning pricing, effectively managing expenses, improving efficiency, and harnessing the power of technology.

The Pursuit of Profitability

As Sarah reflects on her journey as a bookkeeper and entrepreneur, she acknowledges that pursuing profitability has emerged as a recurring motif in her work. With a strong focus on profitability, this entrepreneur has been driven to make strategic decisions and scale her business.

For Sarah, profitability is more than just making money—it's about establishing a sustainable business that can withstand market fluctuations, support her team and clients, and lay the groundwork for long-term success. It's all about striking the perfect equilibrium between income and costs, maximizing effectiveness and efficiency, and providing clients with valuable services that are both profitable and long-lasting.

Optimizing Pricing Strategies

Maximizing profitability can be achieved by optimizing pricing strategies. With a deep understanding of costs, market demand, and competitive pricing, bookkeepers can strategically set prices to maximize revenue while staying competitive.

For Sarah, optimizing pricing strategies was crucial in her quest to maximize profitability. She conducted extensive market research to gain insights into pricing trends and competitive dynamics, considering her overhead costs, labor expenses, and the value she offered to clients. With this information, Sarah could fine-tune her pricing strategy to optimize revenue while providing value to her clients.

Managing Expenses

Like a certified management accountant (CMA), effectively managing expenses is crucial for maximizing profitability. With a keen focus on cost control and efficient spending, bookkeepers can enhance their financial performance and boost their profitability.

For Sarah, effectively managing expenses was always a top priority in optimizing profitability. She diligently established rigorous budgeting and expense-tracking procedures to closely monitor her business's financial well-being and pinpoint opportunities for enhancement. She skillfully negotiated with vendors to secure more favorable pricing and terms while seeking innovative methods to decrease overhead costs without compromising quality or service.

Improving Operational Effectiveness

Optimizing profitability requires a high level of efficiency. With efficient operations, automated tasks, and removing obstacles, bookkeepers can minimize waste and enhance productivity. This enables them to achieve more significant results with fewer resources and ultimately boost their profitability.

For Sarah, maximizing profitability was her top priority as she sought to enhance efficiency. She embraced technology and software solutions to automate routine tasks like data entry, reconciliation, and reporting. This enabled her to save time and concentrate on more strategic activities and value-added services. She also enhanced workflows and processes to eliminate unnecessary steps and streamline operations, improving efficiency and productivity.

Harnessing the power of technology

Technology is essential for bookkeepers to maximize profitability. With the help of software and automation tools, bookkeepers can optimize operations, enhance accuracy, and lower expenses, ultimately boosting their profitability.

For Sarah, harnessing technology was a game-changer in her pursuit of maximizing profitability. She invested in cloud-based accounting software that enabled her to conveniently access client data from any location at any given moment and work together with clients in real time. She also introduced automation tools for tasks like data entry, reconciliation, and reporting, significantly decreasing the time and resources needed to complete these tasks manually.

With a certified management accountant (CMA) expertise, Sarah leveraged technology to enhance efficiency, cut expenses, and ultimately optimize profitability for her business.

Final Thoughts: Achieving Financial Success

As Sarah reflects on her journey to maximize profitability, she understands that achieving success requires dedication, perseverance, and a willingness to adapt to Change. With expertise in financial management, Sarah successfully developed a thriving bookkeeping business that delivered exceptional value to her clients and aligned with her ambitions. As she envisions the future, she understands that maximizing profitability is an ongoing journey—there are always fresh obstacles to conquer, new prospects to pursue, and more outstanding achievements. With her vision, determination, and commitment to excellence, Sarah can consistently increase profitability and accomplish her objectives one step at a time.

7.1 Strategically Pricing Your Services

With expertise in financial management and a deep understanding of the importance of pricing services strategically, one can truly excel in the complex realm of bookkeeping. In this world where numbers hold immense power and value is of utmost significance, navigating pricing with finesse can be the key to surviving and thriving. For bookkeepers like Emily, who are dedicated to establishing long-lasting and lucrative businesses, pricing goes beyond simply choosing a number—it involves comprehending the genuine worth of their services, matching market demand, and optimizing profitability. This sub-chapter will explore the intricacies of strategically pricing your services, examining the factors to consider, the pitfalls to avoid, and practical strategies for success.

Understanding the Value Proposition

Understanding the value proposition is crucial in strategic pricing, as it involves recognizing the distinct benefits and solutions bookkeepers provide to their clients. Emily strives to go beyond the numbers and truly grasp the broader implications of her services on her clients' businesses. It signifies understanding that accounting goes beyond just balancing books and doing calculations—it involves offering reassurance, financial transparency, and valuable insights that enable clients to make informed choices and foster progress.

As Emily looks back on her experience as a bookkeeper, she recognizes that her expertise goes beyond just the services she offers. It's all about her dedication to understanding her client's businesses, the knowledge and insights she brings, and the trust and confidence she instils in them. With a deep understanding of the value she provides, Emily can set prices that accurately reflect the worth of her services and guarantee profitability for her business.

Examining Costs and Overhead

Like a certified management accountant (CMA), a thorough analysis of costs and overhead is essential for strategic pricing and understanding the value proposition. Emily must consider the direct costs of providing her services and indirect costs like overhead, salaries, and administrative expenses. With a deep understanding of the complete cost of operations, Emily can guarantee that her pricing remains competitive in the market while generating profits for her business.

To analyze costs and overhead, Emily meticulously examines her business expenses, such as software subscriptions, office rent, salaries, and insurance premiums. She carefully calculates her break-even point, the minimum revenue required to cover all her expenses. This valuable information guides her in determining the most effective pricing strategy. With a deep understanding of her costs and overhead, Emily can establish prices that cover her expenses and yield a substantial profit margin for her business.

Conducting an in-depth analysis of market dynamics

Researching market dynamics is crucial for strategic pricing. It involves gaining insights into the competitive landscape, recognizing market trends, and assessing client demand. Emily diligently monitors her competitors, comprehends their pricing strategies, and identifies market gaps or opportunities. It also involves staying in tune with the needs and preferences of her target clients and adjusting her pricing accordingly to meet their expectations and deliver value.

Emily stays up-to-date on the latest trends and developments in the industry by conducting market surveys, analyzing industry reports, and attending networking events. She diligently monitors her competitors, carefully observing their pricing strategies and service offerings to maintain her competitiveness in the market. With a deep understanding of market dynamics, Emily can adapt her pricing strategy to take advantage of opportunities and optimize profitability for her business.

Developing Pricing Models that Deliver Value

Creating value-based pricing models is a highly effective strategy for strategic pricing. It involves pricing services based on the perceived value they offer clients rather than just considering the cost of delivering them. Emily's focus goes beyond the hours worked or tasks completed, as she prioritizes the outcomes and benefits her clients gain from her services.

Emily collaborates closely with her clients to understand their objectives, obstacles, and areas of concern. This allows her to customize her services to address their unique requirements and deliver value-based pricing models precisely. She highlights her value, including time savings, enhanced financial clarity, and strategic insights, and sets her prices accordingly.

With a deep understanding of pricing strategies, Emily can effectively position her services as valuable investments for her clients. This approach allows her to set higher prices confidently and boost her business's revenue.

Implementing tiered pricing structures

Implementing tiered pricing structures is an effective strategy for strategic pricing. It allows you to offer different service levels at different prices, catering to clients' diverse needs and budgets. Emily offers various service packages, from basic bookkeeping to comprehensive financial management. The pricing is determined based on the level of service and value provided.

Emily conducts market research to understand the pricing strategies of her competitors and the needs of her target clients, just like a seasoned professional in the field. She then creates a selection of service packages that meet the needs of various client segments, providing a range of features and advantages at different price levels. With the implementation of tiered pricing structures, Emily can broaden her client base, optimize revenue potential, and efficiently meet the varied requirements of her clients.

In conclusion: The Art and Science of Pricing

Emily contemplates her path to strategically pricing her services and acknowledges that pricing requires a careful blend of art and science. It involves comprehending value, assessing costs, studying market trends, and developing pricing models that meet client requirements and standards. With a strategic approach to pricing, Emily can ensure that her services are profitable for her business and valuable to her clients. As she envisions the future, she understands that the path of strategic pricing is far from complete—there are still fresh obstacles to conquer, new prospects to chase, and more outstanding achievements to attain. With her unwavering dedication, exceptional expertise, and unwavering commitment to excellence, Emily is confident in her ability to price her services and achieve her goals strategically, one client at a time.

7.2 Implementing Efficient Time Management Techniques

In the fast-paced world of bookkeeping, where deadlines loom large and tasks pile up quickly, a firm grasp of time management is crucial for success. Bookkeepers, such as Sarah, recognize the importance of efficient time management. It's not just about putting in more effort but about working intelligently, optimizing productivity, and prioritizing tasks to meet deadlines and keep clients happy.

This sub-chapter will delve into the significance of time management for bookkeepers, the typical obstacles they encounter, and practical methods for implementing efficient time management strategies.

The Significance of Effective Time Management

Effective time management is crucial for a bookkeeper's success, going beyond being just a trendy term. With the demands of a fast-paced profession and the importance of precision, mastering time management is crucial for success. It can determine whether deadlines are met, work is high quality, and mistakes are avoided.

Time management is essential for Sarah's daily routine. With her expertise as a certified management accountant (CMA), she knows that her time management skills are crucial in maximizing her productivity, efficiency, and overall success as a bookkeeper. With a deep understanding of effective time management, Sarah excels at staying organized, exceeding client expectations, and achieving a harmonious work-life equilibrium.

Common Challenges in Time Management

Mastering time management can be a daunting task for numerous bookkeepers. Some challenges that people often face include:

Number 1. Bookkeepers frequently experience an overwhelming workload, which can result in stress and burnout.

Number 2. In today's fast-paced world, numerous distractions can hinder our ability to stay focused and productive. From constant email notifications and social media alerts to interruptions from colleagues and clients, it can be challenging to maintain our concentration.

Number 3. Without clear priorities, bookkeepers may jump from task to task, never making progress on the most important projects or delivering subpar work to clients.

Number 4. When planning is not done effectively, it can result in wasted time, missed deadlines, and disorganization, undermining productivity and efficiency.

Practical Techniques for Effective Time Management

Despite these challenges, there are practical techniques that bookkeepers, such as Sarah, can employ to enhance their productivity and time management abilities. Here are a few strategies that can be highly effective:

Number 1. Set clear goals and priorities: Establish clear, attainable objectives for each day, week, and month. Identify the crucial tasks and prioritize them by considering their urgency and importance. By prioritizing important tasks, you can ensure that you progress on essential projects and meet deadlines effectively.

Number 2. Create a daily schedule: Develop a daily schedule or to-do list outlining your tasks and activities. Allocate dedicated time slots for each task, including breaks and smooth transitions between activities. Maintain a strict adherence to your schedule, making necessary adjustments to accommodate any unforeseen changes or emergencies.

Number 3. Stay focused and productive by identifying and eliminating distractions hindering your work. To optimize your productivity, it's essential to minimize distractions. Consider disabling email and social media notifications, establishing clear boundaries with colleagues and clients regarding interruption times, and designating a dedicated workspace free from distractions.

Number 4. Implement Time-Blocking Techniques: You can effectively manage your schedule by dividing your day into blocks dedicated to different tasks or activities. Organize your day by allocating specific time blocks for focused work, client meetings, administrative tasks, and breaks. With this, you'll be able to stay focused and keep up with your goals and a sense of organization.

Number 5. Try practicing the Pomodoro Technique, a time management method that involves working in short, focused bursts followed by short breaks. For 25 minutes, set a timer and do nothing but one task. Once the timer goes off, taking a brief break is essential before starting again. This technique can significantly enhance focus and productivity by breaking tasks into manageable chunks.

Number 6. Figure out obligations which can be delegated to others or automated using technology. Efficiently assign administrative tasks to support staff or virtual assistants and streamline repetitive tasks like data entry, invoicing, and report generation with the help of software tools. Like a certified management accountant (CMA), delegating non-essential tasks allows you to allocate more time to concentrate on high-value activities.

Number 7. Practice effective time management techniques to overcome common challenges and maximize productivity. Through the implementation of strategies like establishing clear objectives and priorities, creating a daily schedule, minimizing distractions, utilizing time-blocking techniques, practicing the Pomodoro Technique, delegating and automating tasks, and employing effective time management techniques, bookkeepers can enhance their efficiency, meet deadlines, and attain tremendous success in their profession.

Conclusion: Becoming a Time Management Expert

As Sarah contemplates the significance of time management in her position as a bookkeeper, she realizes that becoming proficient in time management isn't solely about putting in more effort—it's about adopting a more strategic approach. By implementing practical techniques such as setting clear goals and priorities, creating a daily schedule, minimizing distractions, using time-blocking techniques, practicing the Pomodoro Technique, delegating and automating tasks, and practicing effective time management techniques, Sarah can enhance her productivity, meet deadlines, and achieve tremendous success in her profession. As she envisions the future, she understands that the quest for mastering time management is ongoing—there are always fresh obstacles to conquer, novel strategies to acquire, and exciting prospects to pursue. With her dedication, determination, and commitment to excellence, Sarah is confident in her ability to master the art of time management and achieve her goals, one task at a time.

7.3 Maximizing Efficiency and Boosting Profit Margins through Technology

In the ever-changing world of bookkeeping, technology has become a valuable tool for improving efficiency, simplifying processes, and, ultimately, increasing profits. Emily, a bookkeeper, recognizes the importance of embracing technology to remain competitive and meet clients' needs in today's digital era. In this sub-chapter, we will delve into the significant influence of technology on bookkeeping practices, the essential technologies that enhance efficiency, and practical strategies for utilizing technology to boost profitability.

The Revolutionary Influence of Technology

Technology has completely transformed the bookkeeping profession, encompassing everything from data entry and record-keeping to financial analysis and client communication. Today, bookkeepers have moved away from manual ledger entries and paper-based filing systems. They now rely on various software tools and digital solutions to optimize their operations and offer value to clients.

Emily has found that technology has significantly improved her ability to enhance efficiency and profitability. Emily has leveraged cloud-based accounting software, automated data entry tools, and advanced reporting capabilities to streamline routine tasks, minimize manual errors, and provide her clients with more prompt and precise financial information. Emily's effective use of technology has boosted her productivity and elevated the service she offers to her clients. This has resulted in increased profit margins and greater client satisfaction.

Key Technologies Driving Efficiency Gains

Various cutting-edge technologies are revolutionizing the bookkeeping industry, providing distinct advantages and capabilities to enhance efficiency and boost productivity. Here are some of the most crucial technologies:

Number 1. Cloud-based accounting software, such as QuickBooks Online, Xero, and FreshBooks, enables bookkeepers to conveniently access data from any location and collaborate with clients in real time. These platforms provide advanced features for invoicing, expense tracking, bank reconciliation, and financial reporting, allowing bookkeepers to automate routine tasks and provide more timely and accurate financial information to their clients.

Number 2. Automated data entry tools utilize optical character recognition (OCR) technology to get information from different papers, including receipts and invoices. This data is then automatically populated into accounting software, streamlining the process. These tools streamline data entry, minimizing errors and expediting the reconciliation process.

Number 3. With advanced reporting and analytics tools like Fathom and Spotlight Reporting, you can access robust financial analysis, budgeting, and forecasting capabilities. These tools allow bookkeepers to easily create personalized dashboards and reports, visually analyze financial data, and better understand their clients' businesses. This empowers them to offer valuable strategic advice and guidance.

Number 4. Client communication platforms like Slack and Microsoft Teams enable smooth communication and collaboration between bookkeepers and their clients. These platforms provide messaging, file sharing, and project management functionalities, allowing the bookkeepers to stay connected with clients and promptly address inquiries.

Practical Strategies for Maximizing the Potential of Technology

To fully leverage technology and enhance efficiency and profit margins, bookkeepers such as Emily can employ a variety of practical strategies:

Number 1. Stay current with the latest accounting software and technology advancements by investing in training and education. Take part in workshops, webinars, and gatherings to learn about the newest things. Advancements and expand your knowledge. Additionally, use online resources and tutorials to enhance your proficiency in utilizing technology in your work.

Number 2. Optimize Workflows and Processes: Tailor your workflows and processes to leverage technology's capabilities fully. Identify areas where automation can optimize repetitive tasks, overcome bottlenecks, and establish standardized procedures for utilizing accounting software and other digital tools to ensure uniformity and effectiveness.

Number 3. Integrate Systems and Applications: Integrate your accounting software with other systems and applications to create a smooth workflow. Utilize integrations and APIs to seamlessly connect accounting software with banking, payment processing, and expense management systems. This enables automatic data synchronization and minimizes the reliance on manual data entry.

Number 4. Embrace the power of mobile technology to enhance your efficiency while on the move. Utilize mobile apps for accounting software to access client data from your smartphone or tablet conveniently. Use mobile scanning apps to capture receipts and invoices while on the go effortlessly. By fully embracing the power of mobile technology, you can ensure that you remain highly productive and incredibly responsive, regardless of your location.

Number 5. Streamline Your Workflow: Streamline your workflow by automating routine tasks, which will help you save time and minimize errors. Utilize automated data entry tools to efficiently capture and process receipts and invoices, establish recurring payments, and streamline reminders for overdue invoices. Simplifying repetitive tasks allows you to allocate more time to strategic activities that enhance profitability.

Conclusion: Unlocking the Power of Technology

Emily contemplates the profound influence of technology on her bookkeeping practice and recognizes that maximizing its capabilities is crucial for improving efficiency and profitability. Using cloud-based accounting software, automated data entry tools, advanced reporting and analytics, and client communication platforms, Emily has optimized her operations, provided enhanced value to her clients, and ultimately boosted her profitability.

Emily understands that the ever-changing landscape of technology requires a constant commitment to maximizing its potential. When you think you've mastered it all, there's always something new to discover, fresh tactics to try, and innovative ways to use technology to boost productivity and increase profits. However, with her unwavering dedication, relentless determination, and unwavering commitment to excellence, Emily is confident in her skill to be ahead of the curve and achieve even greater success in her bookkeeping practice.

Chapter 8:

Conquering Obstacles and Avoiding Traps

In the ever-changing realm of bookkeeping, challenges and pitfalls are bound to arise. Like a certified management accountant (CMA), bookkeepers encounter many challenges, from handling client expectations to adapting to regulatory changes. These obstacles can genuinely put their resilience and determination to the test. However, it is frequently by conquering these obstacles that bookkeepers discover growth, knowledge, and, ultimately, achievement. In this chapter, we'll delve into the common challenges and pitfalls that bookkeepers often face and effective strategies for overcoming them. We'll also share valuable lessons learned from real-world experiences.

The Nature of Challenges

For bookkeepers such as Sarah, challenges come in many forms. These problems can have many causes, such as external factors like shifts in tax laws or economic downturns and internal factors like staffing problems or technological disruptions. Like a certified management accountant (CMA), challenges can disrupt workflows, strain client relationships, and impact profitability, regardless of origin.

However, challenges also provide chances for development and creativity. They encourage bookkeepers to think creatively, adapt to new circumstances, and cultivate resilience in facing challenges. As Sarah reflects on her journey, she understands that overcoming challenges has been instrumental in her personal and professional growth. Through these experiences, she has acquired valuable skills, gained new insights, and developed a broader perspective.

Common Challenges and Pitfalls

Bookkeepers often face various challenges and pitfalls:

Number 1. Managing client expectations can be challenging, especially when clients have unrealistic or conflicting demands. Effective communication with clients is crucial for bookkeepers to establish clear expectations, set boundaries, and manage scope creep. All of this helps projects stay on track and within budget.

Number 2. Staying updated on regulatory changes and compliance requirements can be overwhelming, especially in a constantly evolving landscape. Making sure you know about changes in tax rules, accounting standards, and industry regulations is crucial for bookkeepers. It allows them to adapt their practices to ensure compliance and minimize client risk.

Number 3. Technology disruptions can challenge bookkeepers when systems fail or processes break down. Bookkeepers should be ready to address technical problems, establish contingency plans, and remain alert to safeguard confidential client information and ensure uninterrupted business operations.

Number 4. Staffing and Talent Management: Hiring and retaining skilled staff can be challenging for bookkeeping firms, especially in a competitive job market. To attract and retain top talent, bookkeepers must develop effective recruitment strategies, invest in training and Professional growth and make the workplace a good place.

Number 5. Managing work and personal life can be challenging for bookkeepers, particularly during busy tax seasons or when clients are in high demand. Like a certified management accountant (CMA), bookkeepers should prioritize self-care, establish boundaries, and delegate tasks whenever possible to prevent burnout and maintain their overall well-being.

Strategies for Overcoming Challenges

Although challenges and pitfalls are bound to arise, bookkeepers can proactively address them and become stronger. Some good ways to deal with problems are listed below:

Number 1. Communication That Works: Being transparent and honest when you talk to people is crucial for managing client expectations, resolving conflicts, and building trust. Bookkeepers should communicate regularly with clients, actively listen to their concerns, and provide clear project progress and timeline updates.

Number 2. Staying informed about changes in regulations, technology, and best practices in the business is essential to always be ahead of the curve, like a certified management accountant (CMA). Bookkeepers need to prioritize continuous learning and professional development. Taking part in classes is one way to do this. Webinars and conferences. By doing so, bookkeepers can stay informed about the latest industry trends and be better equipped to handle any new challenges that may come their way.

Number 3. Building a solid network of peers, mentors, and industry contacts can provide valuable Support and guidance when facing challenges. It is highly beneficial for bookkeepers to engage in professional associations, networking events, and online communities. These platforms allow individuals to connect in the field, exchange valuable knowledge and experiences, and gain insights from each other's accomplishments and setbacks.

Number 4. Resilience and adaptability are crucial qualities that allow individuals to overcome setbacks and adversity and embrace Change. Bookkeepers can develop resilience and adaptability by adopting a growth mindset, staying positive when confronted with obstacles, and actively pursuing chances to learn and grow.

Number 5. Developing a strategic plan can help bookkeepers anticipate potential challenges and pitfalls and identify proactive measures to mitigate risk and overcome obstacles. Bookkeepers should regularly review and update their strategic plans to remain aligned with the ever-changing business environment. This helps them stay flexible and quick to act, adapting their strategies.

Lessons Learned

As Sarah reflects on her journey of overcoming challenges and pitfalls, she understands that every hurdle she has encountered has provided her with valuable insights that have shaped her into the skilled bookkeeper and entrepreneur she is today. She understands the significance of effective communication in handling client expectations, the need to stay informed and adaptable in a rapidly changing world, and the strength of resilience and perseverance in overcoming challenges.

Above all, Sarah has discovered that obstacles are not barriers but chances for development and Change. They have encouraged her to step outside her comfort zone, think creatively, and become stronger and more resilient. As she looks ahead, she knows she will encounter problems and setbacks. That being said, with the knowledge and experience she has gained,

With her expertise and experience, she is assured that she can conquer any challenge and accomplish her objectives gradually and steadily.

8.1 Common Mistakes to Avoid in a Bookkeeping Business

In the fast-paced world of bookkeeping, where precision and accuracy are crucial, steering clear of common errors can make all the difference in determining your level of success. Emily, a bookkeeper, recognizes the importance of accuracy in managing her clients' finances and maintaining her professional standing. Within this sub-chapter, we will delve into the prevalent errors often made by bookkeepers, the potential consequences of these errors on their business, and practical strategies for preventing them.

1. Ignoring Client Communication

A common mistake many bookkeepers need to make is to talk to their clients. In the fast-paced world of daily tasks and deadlines, it's too familiar to ignore the significance of keeping clients informed and engaged. However, a lack of effective communication with clients can result in misunderstandings, missed deadlines, and, ultimately, lost business.

To prevent this error, bookkeepers should prioritize regular communication with their clients. I ensure regular updates on project progress, promptly address any concerns or questions and establish clear expectations for deliverables and timelines. By maintaining open lines of communication, bookkeepers can establish trust and confidence with their clients, resulting in stronger relationships and increased satisfaction.

2. Ensuring Compliance and Regulations are Not Overlooked

One mistake bookkeeper often make is not paying attention to compliance and legal requirements. Keeping up with the ever-changing tax laws, accounting standards, and industry regulations can take time and effort. Not adhering to legal requirements can lead to fines, penalties, and the possibility of civil action against the bookkeeping business.

To prevent this error, bookkeepers should prioritize continuously keeping abreast of regulatory changes through training, education and compliance requirements. They should also establish robust internal controls and processes to ensure compliance with legal obligations and accurate record-keeping for their clients. With a proactive and vigilant approach, bookkeepers can effectively minimize the risk of compliance-related issues and safeguard their business from potential liabilities.

3. Dependence on Manual Processes

In today's digital age, it can be a costly mistake for bookkeepers to rely too heavily on manual processes. Like a certified management accountant (CMA), traditional bookkeeping methods have become outdated due to their inefficiency, error-proneness, and time-consuming nature. Not adopting technology and automation can impede productivity, restrict scalability, and ultimately affect profitability.

Bookkeepers should embrace technology and use automation whenever feasible to prevent this error. Utilizing cloud-based accounting software, automated data entry tools, and digital payment systems can help streamline workflows and eliminate manual tasks. By fully embracing technology, bookkeepers can enhance accuracy, efficiency, and client service, thus positioning their business for long-term success.

4. Disregarding the dangers of cybersecurity threats

In today's digital age, the ever-present danger of cybersecurity threats cannot be ignored. Businesses constantly battle to protect their sensitive information from data breaches, phishing attacks, and malware infections. Regrettably, numerous bookkeepers fail to recognize the significance of cybersecurity and neglect to establish sufficient measures to safeguard their clients' sensitive information.

- To prevent this error, bookkeepers should prioritize cybersecurity and establish strong security measures to safeguard their data and clients' data against unauthorized access and breaches. Ensuring the highest levels of protection are in place involves utilizing robust passwords.
- They are protecting sensitive data through encryption.
- We are incorporating multi-factor authentication.

- We are consistently updating software and systems to address any potential security weaknesses.

With a focus on cybersecurity, bookkeepers can ensure their business's security and maintain their clients' trust.

5. Neglecting to invest in professional development

Finally, one of the bookkeepers' most common errors is neglecting their professional growth. Like a certified management accountant (CMA), adapting and evolving in a rapidly changing industry is crucial to stay relevant. Not investing in ongoing training and education can restrict growth opportunities, impede career advancement, and ultimately affect the success of the bookkeeping business.

Bookkeepers should prioritize professional development and invest in ongoing learning opportunities to avoid this mistake. This involves participating in workshops, webinars, and conferences, obtaining industry certifications, and seeking guidance and Support from seasoned professionals. Staying informed and up-to-date with the latest trends and developments in the industry can help bookkeepers become trusted advisors to their clients and stand out from the competition.

Final Thoughts: Gaining Wisdom from Errors

Reflecting on common mistakes in a bookkeeping business is crucial for growth and success, as bookkeepers strive to learn from these experiences. By focusing on effective client communication, maintaining regulatory compliance, embracing technological advancements, prioritizing security measures, and investing in continuous professional development, bookkeepers can steer clear of common challenges and position their businesses for sustained success. Although errors can occur occasionally, how bookkeepers handle and grow from these errors ultimately determines their success in the industry.

8.2 Managing Burnout and Maintaining Work-Life Balance

Just like a seasoned professional in bookkeeping, where time is of the essence and client expectations are constant, it is crucial to prioritize self-care and strike a harmonious work-life equilibrium to thrive in the long run. Bookkeepers, such as Sarah, recognized the significance of prioritizing their personal and professional well-being to prevent exhaustion and sustain a sense of job satisfaction.

In this sub-chapter, we'll delve into the common causes of burnout among bookkeepers, the signs and symptoms to be aware of, and practical strategies for effectively managing burnout and maintaining a healthy work-life balance.

Understand Being Burned Out.

Burnout is a disease because of long-term emotional, mental, and physical exhaustion. Stress and excessive workload. It is marked by exhaustion, skepticism, and decreased effectiveness and can significantly impact the person and their job. Bookkeepers often experience burnout due to the demanding nature of their work, strict deadlines, and extended time spent in front of a computer screen.

Identifying the Root Causes of Burnout

Various factors contribute to burnout among bookkeepers:

Number 1. Dealing with a heavy workload is a common challenge for bookkeepers, who often have to manage multiple clients and meet various deadlines. This can create a demanding work environment with constant pressure to deliver results.

Number 2. Working tirelessly and sacrificing personal time is shared among dedicated professionals in the field.

Number 3. Dealing with constant client demands can make it difficult for bookkeepers to establish clear boundaries between work and personal life. This can result in a blurred line between the two and heightened stress levels.

Number 4. Feeling unsupported: Bookkeepers may experience a sense of isolation and lack of Support in their work, especially when working independently or in small firms without a supportive team.

Number 5. Dealing with the ever-evolving world of technology and software updates can overwhelm bookkeepers, often resulting in frustration and inadequacy.

Signs and Symptoms of Burnout

Understanding the indicators and effects of burnout is crucial for taking action promptly and halting any further decline. Here are some common signs and symptoms of burnout:

Number 1. Physical exhaustion can manifest in various ways, such as experiencing chronic fatigue, frequent headaches, and muscle tension. These symptoms are often associated with burnout.

Number 2. Experiencing emotional exhaustion can lead to feelings of irritability, cynicism, and detachment, which are often associated with burnout.

Number 3. Bookkeepers who are experiencing burnout may notice a decrease in motivation and confidence in their job performance.

Number 4. Experiencing burnout can hurt cognitive function, resulting in challenges with concentration, memory, and problem-solving skills.

Number 5. Increased Absenteeism: Individuals in the bookkeeping profession who are dealing with burnout may find themselves taking more sick days or vacation time as a way to manage the symptoms they are experiencing.

Strategies for effectively managing burnout and maintaining a healthy work-life balance although burnout can be overwhelming, it is not unavoidable. Bookkeepers can implement strategies to manage burnout and effectively prioritize life balance.

Here are some strategies:

Number 1. Establishing clear boundaries between work and personal life is crucial. It's essential to define set work hours, schedule regular breaks throughout the day, and consciously unplug from work-related technology during non-work hours.

Number 2. Prioritize self-care by doing things that help you feel good. Physical, emotional, and mental sports, exercise, meditation, and spending time with loved ones are all suitable for your health.

Number 3. When you can, give other people jobs and responsibilities. to lighten your workload and reduce stress. This could include delegating administrative tasks to virtual assistants or working with colleagues on larger projects.

Number 4. Practice Mindfulness: Make mindfulness a part of your daily routine to decrease stress and enhance your awareness of the present moment. Incorporating mindfulness meditation, deep breathing exercises, or regularly pausing and reflecting can be beneficial.

Number 5. Seek Support: Don't hesitate to lean on your network of friends, family members, or colleagues for emotional Support and guidance when needed. You should join a friend support group or look for professional counselling to explore coping strategies and develop resilience, just like someone certified in management accounting.

Number 6. Remember to rest and take breaks throughout the day. Recharge. It may include going for brief walks, practicing relaxation methods, or taking a short break from your workspace to refresh your thoughts.

Number 7. Set realistic goals: Avoid overly ambitious expectations for yourself and your work. Split big jobs into smaller tasks that you can handle. And take the time to acknowledge and appreciate your accomplishments as you progress.

Number 8. Consider Professional Assistance: If you find it challenging to manage burnout by yourself, it may be beneficial to seek professional assistance. A mental health professional can offer help, advice, and techniques for dealing with burnout and enhancing overall well-being.

Final Thoughts: Making Self-Care a Priority

Like a certified management accountant (CMA), bookkeepers recognize the significance of managing burnout and maintaining work-life balance. They know that prioritizing health care is crucial for long-term success and well-being. By implementing healthy work-life balance strategies, bookkeepers can effectively manage burnout and prevent exhaustion. This includes setting boundaries, prioritizing self-care, delegating tasks, practicing mindfulness, seeking

Support, taking regular breaks, setting attainable goals, and getting professional help. Although the profession's demands can be challenging, bookkeepers understand the importance of self-care to maintain personal and professional growth in the long run.

8.3 Adapting to Industry Changes and Economic Shifts

In the dynamic world of bookkeeping, staying adaptable is not optional; it's essential. Emily, a knowledgeable bookkeeper, recognizes the dynamic nature of the industry. She knows the ever-evolving technologies, regulatory demands, and economic fluctuations that influence her work and services. This sub-chapter will delve into the significance of adaptation when confronted with industry changes and economic shifts, the typical challenges bookkeepers encounter when adapting to change, and practical strategies for maintaining agility and resilience in a swiftly evolving environment.

The Significance of Being Adaptable

Adaptation is essential for survival and success in any industry, particularly in the fast-paced world of bookkeeping. In today's fast-paced business environment, bookkeepers must possess the agility and adaptability to navigate technological advancements, regulatory changes, and economic shifts.

Adaptation has been a constant theme throughout Sarah's career as a bookkeeper. Sarah derecognizes the importance of adapting to meet her clients' evolving needs and staying ahead of the curve in a rapidly changing industry. She is well-versed in transitioning to cloud-based accounting software and navigating tax law and regulation changes.

Dealing with the difficulties of adjusting to new circumstances

Adapting to new situations can be challenging at times. Bookkeepers encounter a range of challenges when it comes to adjusting to industry changes and economic shifts, such as:

Number 1. The fast pace of technological innovation can be overwhelming for bookkeepers, especially those who need tech-savvy. Mastering new software and systems, seamlessly incorporating new tools into established workflows, and staying abreast of frequent updates and changes can present a formidable and time-consuming task.

Number 2. Ensuring you're following the rules can be challenging for bookkeepers, especially those working in small firms or as independent practitioners with little Support or resources. Mastering intricate regulatory requirements and guaranteeing compliance can pose a considerable challenge, demanding continuous education and training.

Number 3. During economic uncertainty, bookkeeping businesses may face challenges due to economic shifts like recessions or market downturns. These shifts can significantly impact client demand, revenue streams, and profitability.

Just like a certified management accountant (CMA), bookkeepers must be ready to adjust to shifting economic conditions, broaden their range of services, and seek out fresh avenues for growth and expansion.

Number 4. Client expectations are constantly changing due to technological advancements, shifts in industry trends, and competitive pressures. Proficient bookkeepers should have the foresight to anticipate and fulfil their clients' evolving requirements. They should offer creative solutions and additional services to keep a lead over competitors in the market.

Strategies for Adapting to Change

Like a certified management accountant (CMA), bookkeepers can proactively take steps to adapt effectively to industry changes and economic shifts despite the challenges they may face.

Here are some strategies:

Number 1. Stay up-to-date on changes in technology and regulations, Leveraging industry best practices via ongoing education and career advancement opportunities. Participate in workshops, webinars, and conferences, and utilize resources and training programs to remain current and enhance your skill set.

Number 2. Use technology to help you develop new ideas and work more efficiently rather than being a source of complexity and frustration. Keep up with the latest technologies and fashion styles in the industry. Be open to trying out new tools and systems to enhance productivity and achieve superior outcomes for clients.

Number 3. Stay nimble and adaptable: Cultivate a mindset of flexibility and agility, allowing you to swiftly and effectively adjust to evolving circumstances. Embrace fresh ideas and different viewpoints, and be ready to adapt your strategies and methods to address the changing demands of your clients and the market.

Number 4. Build resilience: Develop the ability to handle and overcome the inevitable setbacks and challenges of adaptation. Emphasize the importance of fostering strong connections with clients and colleagues, maintaining a resilient mindset in challenging situations, and seeking assistance and advice from peers and mentors as necessary.

Number 5. Expand Your Service Offerings: Adapt your services to the evolving needs of your clientele and the market. Discover new areas of expertise, such as virtual CFO services, financial planning, or business advisory services, to set yourself apart from competitors and tap into additional sources of revenue.

Number 6. Connect and Collaborate: Connect and collaborate with peers, industry experts, and other professionals to stay connected and informed about industry trends and opportunities. Engage with professional associations, contribute to online forums and communities, and actively participate in networking events to broaden your connections and stay ahead of industry trends.

Final Thoughts: Embracing Change

Like certified management accountants (CMA), bookkeepers recognize the significance of adjusting to industry changes and economic shifts. They acknowledge that embracing Change is crucial for long-term success and sustainability. With a commitment to continuous learning, embracing technology, and staying agile and flexible, bookkeepers can successfully handle the difficulties in a quickly changing sector. And become stronger and more resilient.

Although adaptation can be challenging at times, bookkeepers understand that it is crucial for staying up-to-date, affluent and competitive in an ever-changing setting.

Chapter 9:

Future Trends in Bookkeeping Like

a savvy business manager, bookkeepers must constantly adapt to the evolving landscape of their profession. It is crucial to proactively stay informed about emerging trends and anticipate the industry's future direction. Throughout this chapter, we will delve into the significant trends that are influencing the future of bookkeeping. These trends encompass many factors, including advancements in technology and automation, evolving client expectations, and the ever-changing regulatory compliance landscape.

By staying informed about these trends and proactively adapting to upcoming changes, bookkeepers can set themselves up for future success.

Embracing the latest technological advancements and leveraging automation

The use of technology is essential for fostering creativity in the bookkeeping industry, and this trend is anticipated to gain even more momentum. The advancements in Machine learning, robotic process automation (RPA), and artificial intelligence (AI) have revolutionized bookkeepers' operations. These technologies automate mundane tasks, allowing bookkeepers to focus on more strategic activities.

We anticipate a higher level of AI and automation in bookkeeping workflows.

Software programs can analyze financial data, detect patterns and anomalies, and provide real-time insights and recommendations. By implementing these changes, efficiency and accuracy can be enhanced, allowing bookkeepers to offer their clients more proactive and value-added services.

Shifts in client expectations

With the ever-changing landscape of technology, client expectations are constantly evolving. In the future, clients will anticipate a higher level of personalized, responsive, and transparent service from their bookkeepers as a result of advancements in digital communication and the increasing need for real-time financial insights.

Bookkeepers should consider embracing digital communication channels, such as video conferencing, messaging apps, and client portals to provide more accessible and timely support to their clients. Investing in tools and technologies that enable real-time financial reporting and analysis is crucial for empowering clients to make informed decisions about their business.

We are ensuring the utmost importance of data security and privacy.

As a business manager, I find it crucial to address the growing concerns surrounding data security and privacy in the face of advancing digitization of financial data. In the future, it will be essential for bookkeepers to prioritize the protection of sensitive client information from cyber threats, data breaches, and regulatory violations.

To Bookkeepers must implement strong security measures to ensure client data security and comply with data protection regulations. These measures may include encryption, multi-factor authentication, and regular security audits. Staying informed about emerging cybersecurity threats and investing in ongoing training and education is crucial for mitigating risks and protecting clients.' interests, just like a business manager would.

The emergence of advisory services is on the rise.

With the rise of automation in bookkeeping, bookkeepers can now dedicate their time and energy to more valuable advisory services like financial planning, budgeting, and business strategy. In the future, there will be a stronger focus on advisory services as bookkeepers establish themselves as trusted advisors and strategic partners to their clients.

Bookkeepers must acquire additional skills and competencies to excel in the evolving landscape of advisory services. These include data analysis, financial modeling, and strategic planning, enabling them to offer valuable insights and recommendations to their clients. It will also necessitate a change in perspective, moving from simply providing services to becoming strategic advisors who offer additional value beyond essential bookkeeping duties.

Globalization

since working remotely has grown more common in today's business landscape.

Remote work and globalization are significant factors influencing the future of bookkeeping. Thanks to advancements in technology and communication, bookkeepers can now work with clients from anywhere globally. This has created exciting prospects for collaboration and growth.

We anticipate an increase in bookkeepers adopting remote work arrangements and expanding their client base beyond geographic boundaries. Adapting to different time zones, cultural norms, and regulatory environments will be necessary, but it will also bring exciting opportunities for growth and diversification.

Inconclusion: Embracing change and innovation

With the ever-changing landscape of the bookkeeping industry shows that significant transformations are taking place. These alterations are motivated by technological advancements, evolving client demands, and shifts in the global

marketplace. By embracing these trends and preparing for the changes, People can set themselves up for success in a quickly evolving landscape.

To succeed in this role; one must be dedicated to constantly learning, being flexible, and thinking outside the box. It's essential to be open to new technologies and approaches to work. Bookkeepers can ensure their survival and success in the years ahead by staying proactive and foreseeing the industry's future trajectory. They can offer invaluable services and perspectives to them clientele, which are essential in forming the profession's future.

9.1 Embracing Automation and Artificial Intelligence

In the world of bookkeeping, automation, and artificial intelligence (AI) are powerful forces reshaping the profession's future. In today's fast-paced in the business landscape, bookkeepers must embrace automation and AI. These technological advancements are no longer optional but essential for staying ahead of the competition, streamlining operations, and providing exceptional value to clients. This section will explore the exciting potential of automation and AI in bookkeeping. We'll discuss how these technologies transform the bookkeeping profession and provide practical strategies for incorporating automation and AI into your practice.

The potential of Automation and AI as a business manager, I know automation and AI have much to offer in bookkeeping. They have the potential to significantly streamline workflows, eliminate manual tasks, and enhance accuracy and efficiency.

With the help of automation and AI technologies, routine bookkeeping tasks can be handled faster and more accurately than humans. These technologies cover everything from data entry and reconciliation to financial analysis and reporting.

One of the main benefits of AI and automation is the time they save for bookkeepers to concentrate on higher-level tasks like financial analysis, forecasting, and advisory services. With the automation of repetitive tasks, bookkeepers can now focus more on delivering value-added services to the clients. This allows them to assist clients in making well-informed decisions and reaching their financial objectives.

Examples of Automation and AI in Bookkeeping

Automation and AI technologies have brought significant changes to bookkeeping industry, transforming the work of bookkeepers and providing valuable advantages to businesses of all sizes.

Here are a few instances were automation and AI are utilized in bookkeeping:

Number 1. Automation tools are handy for streamlining the entering and reconciling of financial data. They can cut down on effort and time considerably. Are needed to input and verify transactions manually.

Number 2. Invoice processing can be streamlined with the help of AI-powered software. This software can extract meaningful information from invoices, like vendor details, invoice numbers, and payment amounts, and enter them into accounting systems with minimal human involvement.

Number 3. Expense management can be streamlined with the help of automation tools that can categorize and process expenses automatically. These tools can also flag unusual or suspicious transactions, allowing bookkeepers to review them further.

Number 4. Financial Analysis: AI algorithms can analyze economic data and uncover trends, patterns, and anomalies. This analysis can offer valuable insights and recommendations, empowering businesses to make well-informed decisions.

Number 5. With the help of AI-powered software, transactions can be monitored in real-time to ensure compliance with regulatory requirements. Any potential issues or discrepancies are promptly flagged for further investigation.

Practical Strategies for Embracing Automation and AI Incorporating automation and AI technologies into their practice effectively can be challenging for bookkeepers despite their clear benefits. Thankfully, there are numerous practical strategies that bookkeepers can employ to embrace automation and AI and maximize their benefits fully:

Number 1. Invest in the Right Tools: Identify automation and AI tools that fit your specific needs and budget, just like a savvy business manager would. Seek out software providers that offer intuitive interfaces, powerful features, and exceptional customer support to facilitate a seamless transition to automated workflows.

Number 2. Start with small tasks that are repetitive and time-consuming, like data entry or invoice processing. By automating these chores, you'll save time and resources.

After becoming proficient in these fundamental processes, gradually incorporate automation into more intricate tasks and workflows.

Number 3. Ensure you give appropriate guidance and assistance to yourself and your team so they can utilize automation and AI tools effectively. Provide opportunities for lifelong learning and career development to stay abreast of the most recent developments in technology and industry best practices in bookkeeping.

Number 4. Collaborate with technology partners and vendors to stay informed about new developments in automation and AI and explore opportunities for customization Its incorporation with the procedures and systems you now use, just like a business manager would.

Number 5. Regularly monitoring the performance of your automated workflows and AI algorithms is crucial for identifying areas that can be improved or optimized. It is essential to be open to adjusting and improving your processes based on feedback and insights from your team and clients.

Number 6. Ensure effective communication with clients by providing regular updates on the advantages of automation and AI. Emphasize how these technologies can enhance efficiency, accuracy, and the overall quality of service. Ensure clear communication regarding updates to your workflows or processes, and offer adequate training and support to guarantee a seamless transition.

Final Thoughts: The Future of Bookkeeping

With the adoption of automation and AI, bookkeepers have the potential to completely transform their work, providing even more value to their clients and playing a significant role in shaping the future of their profession. With automation and AI bookkeepers can enhance workflows, boost efficiency, and provide valuable insights.

This enables them to establish themselves as reliable advisors and strategic allies to their clients, assisting them in reaching their financial objectives and succeeding in a digitalized era. Embracing automation and AI is crucial for staying competitive and leading the way toward a brighter future for the bookkeeping profession.

9.2 The Emergence of Remote Work and Virtual Bookkeeping Services

Over the past few years, remote work has become increasingly popular, revolutionizing the business landscape and transforming how professionals approach their work.

The bookkeeping industry is also experiencing this transformative shift. Given how quickly technology is developing and the sophistication of communication tools, remote work has opened up new opportunities for virtual bookkeeping services.

Within this sub-chapter, we shall examine the elements that have fueled the growth of remote work, the advantages and obstacles of virtual bookkeeping services, and practical approaches to embracing this modern work style.

The Key Factors Influencing Remote Work

Various factors have led to the increase in remote work in the bookkeeping industry and other fields:

Number 1. With technological advancements, bookkeepers can access various digital communication tools, cloud-based software, and collaboration platforms. This enables them to work remotely and easily collaborate with clients from anywhere.

Number 2. Adapting to Evolving Workforce Expectations: The younger generations, immersed in a digital-first environment, are now prioritizing flexible work arrangements to maintain a healthy work-life balance. Remote work provides the freedom and independence that many young professionals seek.

Number 3. Operating across geographic boundaries has become more common for businesses due to the rise of globalization. As a result, bookkeepers must now adapt to different time zones, cultural norms, and regulatory environments.

Number 4. Remote work can provide substantial cost savings for businesses and employees alike. It eliminates the need for office space, commuting expenses, and other overhead costs typically associated with traditional office-based work arrangements.

Number 5. Amidst the pandemic, the COVID-19 outbreak prompted a rapid transition to remote work, compelling businesses to swiftly adjust to remote work settings. Many companies and employees have embraced remote work as a long-term solution, initially driven by necessity.

Advantages of Virtual Bookkeeping Services

Virtual bookkeeping services provide a multitude of advantages for both bookkeepers and their clients:

Number 1. Virtual bookkeeping services offer the advantage of working from anywhere with an internet connection, giving bookkeepers more flexibility and control over their work schedule and location.

Number 2. Virtual bookkeeping services can provide substantial cost savings for bookkeepers and their clients. By eliminating the need for office space and commuting expenses, these services can help businesses save money.

Number 3. Virtual bookkeeping services allow businesses to tap into a global pool of top talent, expanding their options beyond local resources. This presents exciting possibilities for collaboration and innovation on a worldwide level.

Number 4. Virtual bookkeeping services offer the flexibility to adjust to varying client demands, ensuring bookkeepers can swiftly adapt to evolving business needs.

Number 5. Remote work provides increased flexibility and work-life balance, enabling bookkeepers to have more time with their families, pursue personal interests, and eliminate the stress and inconvenience of commuting to and from the office.

The Difficulties of Virtual Bookkeeping Services

Virtual bookkeeping services come with their fair share of benefits, but they also bring along some unique challenges:

Number 1. In a remote work setting, communication can be more difficult because bookkeepers and clients may need more opportunities for face-to-face interaction. Effective communication and regular updates are crucial for fostering strong connections with clients.

Number 2. Remote work poses potential security risks, as sensitive financial data could be vulnerable when accessed and transmitted over unsecured networks. Bookkeepers must establish robust security protocols to safeguard client information from potential cyber threats and breaches.

Number 3. Working with clients from diverse geographic regions and cultural backgrounds can pose challenges such as language barriers, time zone differences, and cultural norms. Bookkeepers must know these differences and adjust them communication and working styles accordingly.

Number 4. Remote work can be isolating, especially for bookkeepers accustomed to working in a team environment. Developing a robust network of colleagues, peers, and mentors can be instrumental in overcoming isolation and gaining valuable support and guidance.

Number 5. Dealing with technical challenges can be frustrating. Remote work heavily depends on technology, and issues like internet outages, software glitches, and hardware failures can wrench your workflow and productivity. Bookkeepers must take a proactive approach to resolve technical problems and reaching out for help when necessary.

Practical Strategies for Embracing Remote Work

Despite the challenges, bookkeepers can utilize various practical strategies to embrace remote work and virtual bookkeeping services effectively.

Number 1. Invest in reliable technology and communication tools that facilitate remote collaboration, such as video conferencing, project management, and cloud-based accounting software.

Number 2. Ensure Effective Communication Ensure effective communication with clients by implementing regular check-ins, providing status updates, and offering channels for addressing any questions or concerns. Establish clear guidelines for how often and how you prefer to communicate.

Number 3. Ensure Data Security Implement strong security measures to safeguard client data from cyber threats and breaches. This includes utilizing encryption, multi-factor authentication, and conducting regular security audits. Inform clients about the most effective methods for safeguarding sensitive information and strongly advocate adherence to security protocols.

Number 4. Build Strong Client Relationships Build strong relationships with clients through trust, transparency, and open communication. Take the initiative to address client concerns and show your dedication to providing top-notch service, even when working remotely.

Number 5. Stay connected with colleagues, peers, and mentors through networking events, online forums, and professional associations to maintain strong professional relationships.

Explore possibilities for collaboration, knowledge sharing, and support from fellow professionals in the industry.

Number 6. Be open to adapting and innovating to meet clients' evolving needs and stay ahead of industry trends. Embrace the latest technologies, tools, and methodologies to provide valuable services and stay ahead in a fast-paced and ever-evolving environment.

Final Thoughts: Embracing the Future of Work

Owing to the increasing acceptance of working remotely and virtual bookkeeping services, bookkeepers can transform their work, provide more value to their clients, and influence the future of their profession. By capitalizing on the advantages of remote work, such as flexibility, cost savings, access to talent, scalability, and work-life balance, bookkeepers can position themselves for success in a rapidly changing industry. Through the strategic implementation of technology and the establishment by establishing effective lines of communication, ensuring the utmost importance is placed on data security, fostering strong connections with clients, maintaining constant contact with colleagues, and embracing adaptability and innovation to meet evolving client demands and industry trends, bookkeepers can excel in a remote work setting and pave the way for a promising future in the field.

9.3 Opportunities for Innovation and Growth in the Industry

Innovation is crucial for the success of any industry, fueling progress, promoting growth, and opening doors to new possibilities for professionals and businesses. As a savvy professional in the bookkeeping industry, one must constantly adapt to the changing landscape and seize opportunities for innovation and growth. This includes embracing emerging technologies and reimagining traditional business models. This sub-chapter will explore various avenues for innovation and expansion in the bookkeeping industry. We will also delve into practical approaches for capitalizing on these opportunities and explore how innovation can bring about significant changes for bookkeepers and their clients.

Embracing the latest advancements in technology

Embracing cutting-edge technology like blockchain, machine learning, artificial intelligence (AI), and robotic process automation (RPA) presents a promising opportunity for innovation and growth in the bookkeeping industry. These technologies can completely transform bookkeepers' operations, making processes more efficient and providing enhanced client value.

AI and machine learning algorithms can automate repetitive bookkeeping tasks like data entry, categorization, and reconciliation. This allows bookkeepers to dedicate their time to more important activities such as financial analysis, forecasting, and providing advisory services. Blockchain technology has the potential to enhance transparency, security, and efficiency in financial exchanges, reducing the likelihood of fraud and error.

With the help of RPA, repetitive processes and tasks like invoice processing and expense management can be automated, leading to improved accuracy and reduced manual labor.

By incorporating these cutting-edge technologies and seamlessly integrating them into their operations, bookkeepers can optimize efficiency, precision, and output, provide added value to their clients, and stand out in a fiercely competitive market.

Introducing New Service Offerings

Expanding service offerings beyond traditional bookkeeping tasks present another excellent chance for growth and innovation in the bookkeeping industry. With clients' ever-changing needs and advancements in technology, bookkeepers currently possess the opportunity to broaden their service offerings. This includes offering financial planning, budgeting, forecasting, business analysis, and advisory services.

Operating with the mindset of a business manager, bookkeepers can offer invaluable guidance and strategic advice to assist companies in reaching their financial objectives and successfully navigating intricate obstacles. With their firm grasp of financial management and a keen understanding of their client's businesses, bookkeepers can provide immense value and become invaluable allies in their clients' journey toward success.

Utilizing the power of data analytics

Data analytics presents an excellent opportunity for innovation and growth in the bookkeeping industry. With the help of data analytics tools and techniques, bookkeepers can gain valuable insights into their client's financial performance. This enables them to recognize patterns and trends. And make informed recommendations to help businesses improve their operations and increase profitability.

Utilizing data analytics, bookkeepers can effectively pinpoint potential risks and opportunities, including emerging market trends, industry disruptions, or financial vulnerabilities. This enables businesses to address these matters and maintain a competitive edge proactively.

By prioritizing data analytics capabilities and developing expertise in data analysis and interpretation, bookkeepers can discover fresh avenues for expansion and set themselves apart from the competition. They can offer valuable insights and recommendations that yield concrete client outcomes.

Embracing a Customer-Focused Strategy

Success in the bookkeeping industry hinges on adopting a client-centric approach, where the primary focus is on comprehending and fulfilling clients' ever-evolving needs in a dynamic marketplace. With an emphasis on prioritizing clients' needs, bookkeepers can uncover fresh possibilities for innovation and expansion, ultimately providing enhanced value.

Regular client surveys and feedback sessions can be conducted to gather insights into clients' pain points, challenges, and priorities. This information can then be used to customize service offerings and solutions to better meet their needs. Building solid relationships with clients is crucial, and this can be achieved through trust, transparency, and open communication. It's essential to proactively address their concerns and expectations to ensure their satisfaction.

Putting the interests of the client first and pledging to surpassing expectations, bookkeepers can cultivate loyalty, enhance satisfaction, and discover fresh avenues for innovation and expansion in the industry.

Practical Strategies for Seizing Opportunities

Taking advantage of opportunities for innovation and growth in the bookkeeping industry necessitates a proactive mindset and a willingness to adapt and try new things. Implementing practical strategies to capitalize on these opportunities are crucial.

Here are a few valuable approaches:

Number 1. Stay updated on the bookkeeping industry's emerging trends and technologies, leveraging best practices via ongoing education and career advancement opportunities. Stay current and expand your skillset by attending workshops, webinars, and conferences and utilizing online resources and training programs.

Number 2. Develop Strategic Partnerships: Work closely with technology partners, industry experts, and other professionals to discover fresh avenues for innovation and expansion. Utilize their knowledge and resources to create cutting-edge solutions and services.

Number 3. Embrace emerging technologies such as AI, machine learning, blockchain, and data analytics to streamline workflows, automate routine tasks, and deliver more value to clients. Discover innovative software tools and platforms to increase output and differentiate oneself in the crowded market.

Number 4. Pay close attention to your client's needs, concerns, and feedback, and utilize this valuable information to customize your service offerings and solutions accordingly. Conduct client surveys and feedback sessions to gather insights into their priorities and expectations. Utilize this valuable information to drive innovation and improvement in your practice.

Number 5. Remain adaptable and open to change to respond to shifts in the market, evolving effectively client demands, and technological advancements. Be open to adjusting your methods and techniques to take advantage of fresh chances and tackle emerging challenges.

Conclusion: Embracing the Opportunities Ahead Curiosity, Creativity and entrepreneurship drive innovation and growth in the bookkeeping industry. With a strategic mindset, embracing emerging technologies, expanding service offerings, harnessing data analytics, and adopting a client-centric approach, and staying agile and flexible in response to change, bookkeepers can seize the opportunities ahead and unlock new possibilities for themselves and their clients. With the ever-changing market landscape, innovation and expansion's potential is unknown. Let's seize the opportunities that lie ahead and work together to shape the future of the bookkeeping industry.

Final Thoughts: Mapping Out the Future of Bookkeeping

As we wrap up this exploration of bookkeeping, it's clear that the field is rapidly changing. With the evolution of technology, the bookkeeping industry has experienced a significant shift from traditional ledger books to modern cloud-based accounting software and virtual bookkeeping services. In this final segment, we will reflect on the main themes and valuable insights we have gained from our exploration and outline a clear path for the future of bookkeeping.

Embracing Change and Innovation

Throughout our exploration, one theme has remained consistent: the significance of embracing change and innovation. The bookkeeping industry is constantly evolving due to technological advancements, client expectations, and changes in the global marketplace. To succeed in this ever-changing landscape, bookkeepers must be flexible, quick on their feet, and willing to embrace fresh concepts, technologies, and approaches to their work.

Since automation and artificial intelligence have become commonplace and the increasing popularity of remote work and virtual bookkeeping services, the industry is ripe with opportunities for innovation and growth. With a strategic mindset and a focus on innovation, bookkeepers can pave the way for future success by staying ahead of industry trends, capitalizing on emerging opportunities, and consistently delivering value to their clients.

Helping clients gain knowledge and take control of their decisions

Bookkeeping is centered around empowering clients through knowledge and understanding. Beyond financial management, bookkeepers play a crucial role as their clients' dependable counselors and strategic partners. They offer valuable insights, recommendations, and guidance to drive business success.

With their firm grasp of financial management, deep industry trends, and knack for deciphering intricate financial data, bookkeepers empower their clients with the necessary insights and resources to make well-informed choices, minimize risks, and attain their financial objectives. By fulfilling this role, bookkeepers contribute significantly to advancing businesses, encouraging creativity, and establishing more robust and adaptable organizations.

Building Stronger Communities Through Collaboration

Collaboration is essential in the bookkeeping profession, as bookkeepers work closely with clients, colleagues, peers, and industry partners to achieve shared objectives and foster collective success. By promoting teamwork and exchanging information, bookkeepers can create more cohesive communities, provide assistance during challenging times, and enhance the overall standing of the profession.

Bookkeepers have numerous opportunities to connect with others in the industry, share insights and best practices, and learn from one another's experiences. These opportunities can arise through networking events, online forums, professional associations, or mentorship programs. Through collaboration and unity, bookkeepers have the power to make a more significant difference, promote their profession, and navigate a shared path toward the future.

Continuing Education and Professional Development

As a professional in bookkeeping, staying informed and continuously learning is essential. Like a business manager, bookkeepers must constantly refresh their expertise and capacity to stay updated with the latest accounting software and changes in tax laws and regulations.

By actively developing their skills, broadening their knowledge base, and proactively pursuing opportunities for growth and advancement, bookkeepers can stay ahead of the competition and maintain their position as industry leaders. Bookkeepers have numerous opportunities to enhance their knowledge and expand their skills through formal education, certifications, workshops, or online courses.

A Promising Future Ahead

When considering the future of bookkeeping, it becomes evident that the possibilities are limitless. With the ability to embrace emerging technologies and expand service offerings, bookkeepers can shape the future of their profession and significantly impact the businesses and individuals they serve.

Bookkeepers can create a meaningful difference by fostering stronger client relationships and building stronger communities.

In a world that is changing quickly, success requires bookkeepers to be open to change, encourage innovation, and uphold their values of integrity, professionalism, and excellence. Bookkeepers are essential contributors to the global economy, using their expertise to shape the future of businesses through meticulous financial management.

In summary

As we conclude this exploration, it is evident that bookkeepers have a significant influence on the businesses, organizations, and individuals they assist. With their expertise in financial management, bookkeepers are instrumental in maintaining the economic well-being of businesses, enabling them to thrive and reach their objectives.

Like a business manager, the bookkeeping industry constantly evolves and adapts to suit the market demands of clients and the marketplace. However, one thing that always stays the same is the crucial role of bookkeepers in maintaining financial stability, transparency, and accountability. With a strategic mindset and a forward-thinking approach, bookkeepers have the power to drive success and shape the future of their profession for years to come. By embracing change, fostering innovation, and staying true to their core values, they can chart a course for long-term growth and prosperity.

As we conclude this exploration of bookkeeping, let's remember the valuable lessons, insights, and connections we've made. We will use these to navigate the dynamic world of the bookkeeping profession. As a business manager, I know that the future of bookkeeping is filled with promise and driven by determination, passion, and a relentless pursuit of excellence.

Reflecting on Your Journey: Celebrating Milestones and Successes

As we conclude this exploration into bookkeeping, it is crucial to pause, contemplate, and commemorate the milestones and accomplishments attained throughout this journey. As a bookkeeper, every success, no matter how small, is a meaningful milestone on the journey toward professional growth and achievement. As a business manager, it is crucial to take the time to reflect on your trip, acknowledge and celebrate milestones and successes, and recognize the profound impact these moments can have on your motivation, confidence, and sense of fulfillment.

Reflecting on one's actions and experiences is crucial for personal and professional growth.

Reflection is an invaluable tool for personal and professional development, enabling individuals to gain valuable insights, learn from previous experiences, and plan for the future. In the dynamic realm of bookkeeping, where time is of the essence, and expectations are relentless, it is crucial to carve out moments for introspection and contemplation of your professional path.

Reflection enables you to:

Number 1. Reflecting on your journey allows you to acknowledge and celebrate the achievements, milestones, and successes you have accomplished. Whether securing a new client, successfully finishing a demanding project, or obtaining a professional certification, every accomplishment signifies a noteworthy milestone in your career as a bookkeeper.

Number 2. Reflection also helps you identify areas for growth and improvement so you can learn from your mistakes, challenges, and setbacks. Through careful analysis of previous experiences, one can acquire valuable insights into practical strategies, areas for improvement, and potential avenues for even greater success in the future.

Number 3. Reflecting on your journey can reignite your motivation and passion for your work, reminding you of why you chose to pursue a career in bookkeeping in the first place. Like a successful business manager, this can help you stay focused and driven. By reflecting on your achievements and triumphs, you can access the feeling of purpose and satisfaction that arises from positively influencing the businesses and individuals you assist.

Number 4. Reflection is crucial for maintaining perspective. It allows you to step back from the daily grind and gain a broader view of the situation. By evaluating your progress and accomplishments, you can gain a fresh perspective and clear direction as you move forward.

Recognizing Achievements and Reaching Goals

Like a business manager, reflecting on your progress and celebrating milestones and successes is essential. This helps acknowledge your achievements, uplift team spirit, and foster a positive environment at work. Recognizing and commemorating significant accomplishments, whether individual achievements, team successes, or essential project milestones, is crucial for maintaining motivation, engagement, and job satisfaction.

Recognizing and commemorating achievements enables you to:

Number 1. Recognize Hard Work and Dedication: Commemorating milestones and accomplishments acknowledges the immense effort, commitment, and dedication you and your team have invested in attaining your objectives. This is an opportunity to recognize the extensive amount of time dedicated to working diligently on spreadsheets, managing accounts, and ensuring accurate financial statements.

Number 2. Recognizing achievements and milestones can positively impact team morale and motivation. It can inspire you and your team to take on new challenges and aim for tremendous success. It serves as a reminder of the rewards from dedication and the recognition and gratitude you receive from those in your circle.

Number 3. Building Confidence and Self-Esteem: Celebrating milestones and successes fosters a strong sense of pride and accomplishment, boosting confidence and self-esteem. It serves as a confirmation of your abilities, talents, and expertise as a bookkeeper. It serves as a reminder that you can accomplish anything you want.

Number 4. Creating a Positive Work Environment: Finally, acknowledging achievements and milestones helps create a work environment that values and promotes recognition, appreciation, and teamwork. It fosters unity and camaraderie among team members, strengthening their bonds and developing a deep sense of belonging and community.

Practical Strategies for Recognizing Achievements and Reaching Milestones

Recognizing achievements and accomplishments doesn't have to be extravagant or expensive—it can be as easy as expressing gratitude, giving applause, or writing a thoughtful note of appreciation.

There are numerous methods to acknowledge and commemorate accomplishments in your bookkeeping practice, such as:

Number 1. Consider implementing a recognition program or organizing an awards ceremony to honor exceptional performance, accomplishments, and contributions. Acknowledge individuals or teams who have shown outstanding commitment, creativity, or collaboration, and express gratitude by presenting them with certificates, plaques, or other forms of recognition.

Number 2. Host team celebrations or social events to celebrate significant milestones, project completions, or team successes. Organizing team events, such as team lunches, happy hours, or virtual get-togethers, can help strengthen the bond among team members and create a sense of unity.

Number 3. Personalized Recognition: Make sure to take the time to personalize recognition and appreciation efforts, tailoring them to the preferences and interests of each team member. Implementing various forms of personalized recognition, such as thank-you note, small gifts, or public acknowledgments during team meetings, demonstrates a genuine appreciation for the individual contributions of each team member.

Number 4. Publicly recognizing achievements and successes is essential for keeping everyone informed and motivated. Social media, newsletters, and company-wide announcements can all be used for this.

Posts. Emphasize personal achievements, team goals, and client victories, and commemorate the overall accomplishments of your bookkeeping practice.

Number 5. Consistent Feedback: Offer regular feedback and recognition consistently rather than solely focusing on significant milestones or accomplishments. It is essential to consistently recognize and value your team members' hard work and contributions. Additionally, offering constructive feedback can assist them in their professional growth and development.

Final Thoughts: Embracing Your Progress

As we conclude this journey, we must pause and acknowledge the significant milestones and achievements that have defined our progress as bookkeepers and professionals; every achievement, whether small or big, signifies progress.

As we take a moment to pause, it's essential to reflect on and appreciate the hard work, dedication, and passion that have led us to this point. As we reflect on our journey, it's essential to recognize the obstacles we've conquered, the valuable insights we've gained, and the progress we've made. Let's maintain the spirit of celebration, gratitude, and appreciation as we move forward, aiming for excellence and creating a positive impact in the bookkeeping industry.

Looking Ahead: Sustaining Success in Your Bookkeeping Goldmine

As we approach the conclusion of our journey through the realm of bookkeeping, let us now turn our attention to the future and imagine what lies ahead. The path of a bookkeeper is constantly changing, offering chances for advancement, creativity, and achievement.

This final section will explore practical strategies to ensure ongoing success in your bookkeeping business. We will discuss how to navigate challenges, seize opportunities, and create a path toward long-term fulfillment in your career. Adopting an attitude of lifelong learning and career advancement is crucial for personal and career growth.

To thrive in the ever-evolving bookkeeping industry, it is crucial to prioritize ongoing learning and professional development. To stay ahead in the ever-changing world of bookkeeping, it is essential for professionals to continuously enhance their skills, broaden their knowledge, and keep up with the latest industry trends and best practices.

Practical strategies for embracing continuous learning and professional development involve:

Number 1. Consider pursuing advanced training by enrolling in courses, workshops, or certification programs. These opportunities can help you deepen your expertise in specific areas of bookkeeping, such as tax preparation, financial analysis, or industry-specific accounting principles.

Number 2. Attending Industry Events: Participate in industry conferences, seminars, and social gatherings to keep abreast of the newest developments, technologies, and regulatory developments in the bookkeeping profession. Going to these events might establish a connection with colleagues, gain insights from seasoned professionals, and broaden your professional circle.

Number 3. Looking for Mentorship: Find mentors or advisors who can offer guidance, support, and mentorship as you progress in your bookkeeping career. Having a mentor can be incredibly beneficial. They can provide insightful commentary, relate personal stories, and provide suggestions for overcoming obstacles and accomplishing your goals.

Number 4. Utilizing Online Resources: Make the most of online resources like webinars, podcasts, and online forums to stay up-to-date on the latest industry trends and developments. These resources provide convenient and accessible ways to improve your abilities and understanding from home.

By dedicating themselves to lifelong study and career advancement, bookkeepers can proactively stay ahead of industry trends, adjust to evolving market dynamics, and establish themselves as reliable consultants and authorities.

Embracing innovation and technology

Maintaining a competitive edge requires embracing innovation—an edge in bookkeeping. With a strategic mindset, bookkeepers can tap into the potential of cutting-edge technologies, explore fresh business models, and implement creative methods to enhance their service delivery. This will open up exciting avenues for growth and set them apart from the competition.

Implementing practical strategies to embrace innovation and technology is essential for keeping up with today's fast-paced business world. Landscape. Some valuable approaches to consider include:

Number 1. Investing in Automation: Embrace automation tools and software solutions to streamline repetitive tasks, improve efficiency, and reduce manual errors in your bookkeeping practice. Efficient processes like data entry, invoicing, and expense tracking can optimize time and allocate resources for more strategic endeavors.

Number 2. Optimizing Cloud-Based Solutions: Embrace the power of cloud-based accounting software and tools to gain immediate access to financial data, foster seamless collaboration with clients, and fortify the security and dependability of your bookkeeping operations. Cloud-based solutions provide the ability to scale, adapt, and access work from anywhere and anytime, making it convenient for bookkeepers.

Number 3. Utilize data analytics tools and techniques to better understand your client's financial performance. Identify trends and patterns in the data and provide data-driven recommendations to help businesses improve their operations and increase profitability. Utilizing data analytics, bookkeepers can effectively identify potential risks and opportunities, allowing companies to take proactive measures and maintain a competitive edge.

By embracing innovation and technology, bookkeepers can stand out in a competitive market, provide more value to their clients, and set themselves up for long-term success and expansion.

Developing and preserving solid client relationships is essential for success in any business. Businesses can foster long-term partnerships and drive growth by prioritizing client satisfaction and consistently delivering exceptional service. Effective communication, active listening, and a genuine interest in understanding clients' needs are crucial to nurturing these relationships. Additionally, regularly seeking feedback and proactively addressing any concerns.

Building solid and trusted relationships with clients is essential in bookkeeping. Bookkeepers can cultivate loyalty, trust, and satisfaction among their clientele by deeply understanding their clients' needs, offering tailored service, and delivering outstanding value.

Implementing practical strategies to foster strong client relationships:

Number 1. Offer proactive advisory services to assist clients in reaching their financial objectives and overcoming obstacles, going beyond the typical responsibilities of a bookkeeper. Operating with a mindset akin to that of a business manager, one can enhance client relationships and set their practice apart from competitors by providing services with additional value, including budgeting fin, financial planning, and strategic advice.

Number 2. Effective Communication: Ensure clear and transparent communication with clients, providing regular updates on their financial status, deadlines, and any significant changes or updates. Consistent communication and frequent updates are essential for establishing trust and confidence in your services.

Number 3. Consistently showcase the worth of your services to clients by providing precise, prompt, and dependable financial information, insights, and recommendations. Demonstrate to clients the impact of your expertise and guidance on their goals and economic performance.

Number 4. Requesting Feedback: Regularly ask clients for feedback to assess their satisfaction with your services and pinpoint areas that can be enhanced. Listen attentively to their concerns, suggestions, and feedback, and take prompt action to resolve any issues or problems. Through strong client relationships, bookkeepers can establish a dedicated client base, foster repeat business, and garner new clients through positive word-of-mouth referrals and glowing reviews.

Final Thoughts: Succeeding in Your Bookkeeping Goldmine

Looking towards the future of bookkeeping, it's evident that there are endless possibilities for growth, innovation, and success. With a mindset focused on development and improvement, an openness to new ideas and advancements, a dedication to building strong connections with clients, and a commitment to upholding your guiding principles, you can ensure ongoing success in your bookkeeping endeavors.

And reach your desired outcomes.

As you continue your journey as a bookkeeper, it's essential to maintain a sense of curiosity, adaptability, and a solid commitment to providing exceptional value to your clients and community. With a professional mindset and a focus on success, there are endless possibilities for what can be accomplished in the ever-evolving field of bookkeeping. You are wishing your ongoing success and prosperity in the years ahead!

Appendix: More Tools and Resources for Bookkeepers

This appendix has compiled a complete list of extra resources, tools, and references to help bookkeepers with their practice and career growth. These tools are meant to help bookkeepers stay up-to-date, improve their skills, and do well in their jobs. They include educational materials, training programs, software tools, and industry groups.

1. Resources for learning

- **Online Courses and Training Programmed:** You can find a lot of courses on Coursera, Udemy, and LinkedIn Learning, among other sites, that teach budgeting, basic accounting, tax preparation, and financial analysis. These classes give you a lot of different ways to learn, and they cover topics that are important for all levels of bookkeepers.

- **Professional Certification Programmed:** Think about getting professional certifications like Certified Bookkeeper (CB) or Certified Public Bookkeeper (CPB) from groups like the National Association of Certified Public Bookkeepers (NACPB) or the American Institute of Professional Bookkeepers (AIPB). These qualifications can help your professional standing by showing that you are an expert and trustworthy bookkeeper.

- **Publications and journals in the accounting and bookkeeping fields:** To get the latest news, views, and trends, subscribe to magazines and journals, such as The Journal of Accountancy, Accounting Today, or The CPA Journal. These publications give bookkeepers helpful information about changes in the business, new rules, and the best ways to do their jobs.

2. Tools and programs for software

- **Accounting Software:** Look into QuickBooks, Xero, and FreshBooks as possible accounting software options for keeping track of costs, managing transactions, and making financial reports. These software programs have easy-to-use interfaces, many useful features, and choices that can be changed to fit the needs of bookkeepers' and clients' needs.

- **Time Tracking and Billing Tools:** To keep track of billable hours, handle client projects, and make billing more accessible, you might want to use time tracking and billing software like TSheets, Harvest, or FreshBooks. These tools help bookkeepers keep accurate records of their time and costs to bill and process timely payments.

- **Document Management Systems:** Use Dropbox, Google Drive, Evernote, or another document management system to keep client papers, receipts, invoices, and financial records safe in the cloud. These systems make accessing files from any device effortless and help bookkeepers effectively track client information.

3. Professional groups and organizations for networking

- **American Institute of Professional Bookkeepers (AIPB):** Join professional groups like AIPB to get access to resources, networking opportunities, and training programs made just for bookkeepers. The AIPB helps bookkeepers improve their skills and careers by providing certification programs, workshops, and networking events.

- **National Association of Certified Public Bookkeepers (NACPB):** If you are a certified public bookkeeper, you can access certification programs, continuing education courses, and industry tools by becoming a member of NACPB. Bookkeepers and experts in the field can meet with each other through NACPB's online forums, discussion groups, and networking events.

As a bookkeeper, you can meet other people in your area through local networking groups, meetups, or professional clubs and share your knowledge and ideas with them. Bookkeepers at all stages of their careers can benefit from these networking events because they offer help, guidance, and chances to work together.

4. Resources for Regulatory and Compliance

The Internal Revenue Service (IRS) says you can stay current on tax laws, rules, and filing requirements using the IRS's tools and publications. The IRS website has information on how to file your taxes when the deadlines are, and what companies and individuals need to do to become

- **State Boards of Accountancy:** Check with your state's board of accountancy or regulatory body to find out what bookkeepers need to do to get a license, how many CPE credits they need, and what the professional standards are in your state. These groups give advice and tools to ensure that state laws and moral standards are followed.

- **Financial Accounting Rules Board (FARB):** Use FARB's resources and publications to stay current on accounting rules and principles. You can find codifications of accounting standards, implementation guides, and learning materials on the FARB website. These include materials about recognizing income, accounting for leases, and financial reporting.

5. Online chat rooms and forums

- **Reddit:** Join subreddits about bookkeeping, like r/bookkeeping or r/Accounting, to talk about bookkeeping topics, get answers to your questions, and get help from other users. Bookkeepers and accountants with a lot of experience share information, tips, and ideas on these online communities.

- LinkedIn Groups: Join LinkedIn groups like Bookkeepers Network or Accounting and Bookkeeping Professionals to meet other people in the field, get news about the profession, and discuss the best ways to do bookkeeping. People in these groups can share their thoughts, ask questions, and contact other professionals in the same area.

Final Thoughts

In conclusion, the appendix is a valuable tool for bookkeepers who want to learn more, get better at what they do, and keep up with changes and trends in the business. Bookkeepers can continue to do well in their jobs and provide excellent value to their clients and the community through online forums, professional groups, software tools, educational resources, and regulatory resources. No matter how long you've been a bookkeeper or just starting, these tools can help you learn, grow, and advance your career in the exciting and rewarding field of bookkeeping.

Sources for Additional Learning and Professional Growth

To have a successful job as a bookkeeper, you need to keep learning and growing as a professional. In accounting, a field that changes quickly, it's essential to keep up with the latest trends, rules, and tools to stay relevant and give clients good services. Today, we will discuss some of the tool's bookkeepers can use to learn more and grow as professionals.

1. Training and courses you can take online

Bookkeepers can learn new things and improve their skills flexibly and efficiently through online classes and training programs. Whether you want to learn more about basic accounting, discover new software tools, or delve into more specialized areas like tax preparation or financial analysis, many courses can help you.

Many classes on platforms like Coursera, Udemy, and LinkedIn Learning are related to bookkeeping and accounting. These classes are usually given by professionals in the field and cover everything from bookkeeping basics to more advanced methods and ways to be successful. There are also certification choices for many courses, which can help you show clients and employers that you are knowledgeable and trustworthy.

2. Programs for professional certification

Professional certification programs give bookkeepers a way to get official credit for their skills and knowledge. In the field, certifications like Certified Bookkeeper (CB) or Certified Public Bookkeeper (CPB) are well-known and can help bookkeepers stand out.

The National Association of Certified Public Bookkeepers (NACPB) and the American Institute of Professional Bookkeepers (AIPB) have qualification programs for bookkeepers. Usually, people who want to get into these programs must pass a test covering basic accounting, managing payroll, and preparing taxes. Getting a certification shows that you are dedicated to doing your best and can lead to new career possibilities.

3. Publications and journals in the industry

To stay ahead of the curve, bookkeepers need to know about changes in the law, business trends, and best practices. Journals and publications in the field offer bookkeepers valuable insights and details on various vital issues.

Accounting professionals can read articles, case studies, and research in journals like The Journal of Accountancy, Accounting Today, and The CPA Journal. These journals cover many themes, including changes to tax laws, technology trends, and business strategies. By reading these magazines, bookkeepers can stay updated on the latest changes in the field and learn valuable skills they can use in their work.

4. Workshops and webinars

Webinars and workshops are fun and involve ways for bookkeepers to learn from thought leaders and experts in their field. These sessions, which can be live or recorded, cover a wide range of topics, from business management techniques to technical skills.

Professional groups, software companies, and industry groups put on a lot of lectures and workshops for bookkeepers. These meetings often include case studies, demonstrations, and Q&As so that people can get real-world advice and ask questions immediately. Bookkeepers can stay current on new technologies and trends and meet with others through webinars and workshops.

5. Conferences and events for networking

Bookkeepers can meet other bookkeepers, share ideas, and learn from leaders in the field at networking events and workshops. A lot of the time, these events have keynote speakers, panel discussions, and breakout sessions with a lot of different themes that bookkeepers will find helpful.

Professional groups, business groups, and software companies often hold conferences and events for bookkeepers to meet others in their field and network. You can meet other professionals in the same field at these events, make connections, and grow your career network. Attending conferences and networking events can also help you learn about new growth and development chances, best practices, and industry trends.

Final Thoughts

In conclusion, bookkeepers can find many tools to help them learn more and grow as professionals. You can find ways to understand what works for you and your schedule, such as online classes, certification programs, industry magazines, webinars, and networking events. Bookkeepers can use these tools to stay current on the latest technologies and trends, improve their skills, and set themselves up for job success. To do well in the exciting and satisfying field of bookkeeping, you need to keep learning and growing as a professional. These resources will give you the tools and support to reach your goals.

Sample Templates and Documents for Running a Bookkeeping Business

To run a good bookkeeping business, you must keep things organized and running smoothly. Having the proper templates and papers can make things go faster, correctly, and professionally. In this part, we will look at some sample templates and documents that bookkeepers can use to run their businesses more efficiently.

1. Documents for welcoming clients

Getting helpful information and setting clear expectations before taking on new clients is essential.

Here are some examples of templates for papers that welcome new clients:

- **Client Intake Form:** This form asks for general information about the client, like the business's name, how to reach them, and how the company is set up. It might also ask about their favorite accounting software, their financial goals, and any problems they're having.

- **Engagement Letter:** An engagement letter spells out the services offered, how much they will cost, and any other rules and guidelines governing the engagement. It ensures that everyone is on the same page and keeps the cashier from having to deal with misunderstandings or disagreements in the future.

- **Privacy Policy:** This tells the bookkeeper how to handle the client's private data and secret information. It helps the client and bookkeeper trust each other and be honest.

2. Templates for Financial Reporting

Financial reporting must be clear and accurate so clients can understand their economic success and make intelligent decisions.

Here are some examples of templates for business reports:

- **Balance Sheet Template:** A balance sheet template shows the client's assets, bills, and equity at a certain point, giving a snapshot of their financial situation. It helps clients determine how healthy their finances are and how open and solvent they are.

- **Income Statement Template:** An income statement template shows how much money the client made, how much they spent, and their net income or loss for a certain period, like a month, quarter, or year. It helps clients keep track of their profits and find places where they can do better.

- **Cash Flow Statement Template:** A cash flow statement template tracks how much money comes in and goes out of a client's business, investments, and loans. It helps clients keep track of their money and plan for future costs.

3. Invoices and other billing paperwork

To keep cash flow and ensure clients pay on time, sending out invoices quickly and correctly is essential.

Here are some examples of invoice and payment templates:

- **"Invoice Template":** An invoice template has information like the client's name and contact information, a list of the services offered, the amount and price of each service, and the total amount due. It gives you a professional, standard way to bill your clients.

- **Payment Reminder Template:** A payment reminder template contacts clients whose bills are still due. It is a friendly reminder that the payment is late, a summary of the amount still owed, and directions on how to make the payment.

- **Receipt Template:** A receipt template shows that you've gotten payment from a client. The cash amount, date, method of payment, and a reference number for tracking are all written on it.

4. Project management and time-tracking forms

Time tracking and project management that work well are necessary to get the most work done and make the most money.

These are some examples of forms for managing projects and keeping track of time:

- **Timesheet Template:** A timesheet template helps bookkeepers keep track of the hours they can bill for each client or job. It has spaces for writing down the date, the start and end times of the work, an account of the work, and the total number of hours worked.

- **Project Plan Template:** A project plan template spells out the project's goals, deliverables, schedule, and scope. It helps bookkeepers keep track of everything and ensure everything gets done on time and budget.

- **Task Checklist Template:** A task checklist template lists the steps needed to finish a job or task. Bookkeepers can set priorities, stay on task, and ensure nothing gets missed with this tool.

5. Materials for marketing and branding

It would help if you had strong marketing and branding to get new customers and build a good image in your field.

Here are some examples of forms for marketing and branding materials:

- **Business Card Template:** A bookkeeper's name, contact details, and logo are on a business card template. It's a professional way to meet possible clients and work partners and make an impression.

- **Brochure Template:** A brochure template shows off the bookkeeper's services, skills, and what they can do for you. It is a marketing tool that helps potential clients learn about the benefits of working with the bookkeeper.

- **Social Media Post Template:** A social media post template gives you a structure for writing engaging and useful LinkedIn, Facebook, and Instagram posts. It lets bookkeepers show off their skills, share helpful information, and connect with the people they want to communicate with.

Final Thoughts

To sum up, sample templates and papers are valuable tools bookkeepers can use to streamline their work, make it more professional, and make their business run more smoothly. Having suitable templates for things like marketing and branding materials, financial reporting templates, invoicing and billing documents, time tracking, project management documents, or documents for onboarding new clients can save you time, reduce mistakes, and make your clients happy.

By using sample templates and papers, bookkeepers can ensure clients know what to expect, give accurate and timely financial reports, ensure invoices are sent out quickly and correctly, increase productivity and profits, and market their services effectively to get new clients. No matter how long you've been an accountant or how new you are to the job, these templates can help you run a successful business.

NOTE: Index

The index is like a plan that helps readers find the book's specific ideas, topics, and data. It gives a complete list of all the keywords, terms, and issues discussed in the text, along with the page numbers where more information can be found. Even though it's often forgotten, the index makes the book more straightforward and accessible. It helps readers find the necessary information quickly and easily explore the text.

We'll talk about what the index means and how it helps readers get the most out of the book's material here. We'll also talk about how to make an index that does an excellent job of showing what the book is about and meets the needs of its readers.

1. How Important the Index Is

The index benefits people looking for specific information or topics in a book. It can be searched like a library, so people can quickly find what they're looking for without reading the whole thing. The index makes it easy for readers to find the information they need, whether they are looking for a specific idea, term, or case study. This saves them time and effort.

In addition, the index makes the book more straightforward to use and find, which makes it more reader- and user-friendly. The index allows readers to interact with the material in a way that fits their needs and interests by putting it in a structured and searchable format. The index makes it easier for readers to find their way around the book, whether they like to read from beginning to end or jump around to different parts.

The index helps readers and is an excellent resource for researchers, academics, and people working there. The index makes it easy for scholars to find specific information for citing, analyzing, or doing more research by giving a complete list of subjects and references. Also, it ensures that many people can read and find the book's content, which adds to its effect and influence in the field.

2. Parts of an Index That Works

To make a good index, you must plan, organize, and pay close attention to the details. When creating an index for your book, here are some essential things to keep in mind:

- Keywords and Terms: List the most important ideas, words, and subjects that readers will likely be interested in. These terms are like entrances to the index; they lead readers to the right parts of the text.

- Subentries and Cross-References: Put the index entries into groups and subentries organized in a hierarchy to make the structure make sense and more accessible to find your way around. Cross-referencing similar words or topics will help readers learn how different ideas and concepts are connected.

- Page Numbers: Make sure that each index entry has a correct page number so readers can quickly find the material referred to in the book. Check the page numbers twice to make sure they are correct, and if they need to be changed, do so during the last round of editing.

- **Formatting and Style:** Use the same formatting and style rules throughout the index to make it easier to read and use. Use bold or italicized text to draw attention to main and sub-entries, and keep your writing simple and to the point to get your point across quickly.

- **Include everything:** Ensure the index includes everything about the book and all the essential ideas, concepts, and themes. Look over the table of contents, chapter titles, and subheadings to find possible index entries and ensure all the information is covered.

User-Friendly Design:

1. Make the index easy to use by putting usefulness and accessibility first.
2. Use an easy-to-understand layout with items set up by letter or theme to make them quick and easy to find.
3. Consider adding a detailed index to the end of each chapter or part so readers can quickly find the information they need.

3. Tips for Making an Effective Index

A systematic and thorough technique is needed to make an excellent index. When creating an index for your book, here are some things to think about:

Starting early is essential. Plan and make the index as soon as the text is almost finished. Look over the chapter summaries and table of sections to find significant ideas and topics that should be in the index.

- **Work with Others:** Get help and input from coworkers, editors, or experts in the field to ensure the index correctly describes the content and meets the intended audience's needs. Make an index advisory board or hire a skilled indexer to help you.

- **Use Indexing Software:** Use the tools and apps with indexing software to make the indexing process easier and faster. These tools have features like automatic page numbering, keyword tagging, and format choices that can be changed to help you make an index that looks professional.

- **Review and Revise:** Once the first draft of the index is finished, carefully review it to ensure it is correct, complete, and consistent. Ensure everything is right by repeatedly checking the page numbers, cross-references, and style. Ask beta readers or writers for feedback to find any holes or places where you can improve.

- **Iterate and update:** Indexing is an iterative process, and it may take more than one round of revisions to make a complete and well-written index. You should be ready to make changes to the index based on what users and other important people say, and you should update it as needed to reflect any changes or additions to the book's content.

4. In conclusion

In conclusion, the index is essential to any book because it helps readers find specific information quickly and easily. The index makes the book more straightforward to use, more accessible, and more enjoyable to read by putting the material into a structured and searchable format. It takes careful planning, organization, and attention to detail to make a good index, but the work is well worth it so readers can get the most out of the book. You can make your book more valuable and useful for readers for years if you put in a well-written index, whether you're the author, editor, or publisher.

www.ingramcontent.com/pod-product-compliance
Lightning Source LLC
Chambersburg PA
CBHW052240220526
45471CB00001B/125